Jennifer LeClaire has don[...] cannot survive without an Ahab spirit that gives the demonic authority to operate. In this work Jennifer LeClaire strips away the veneer of satanic liars and religious counterfeits to expose and expel this hindering spirit. I commend this to all who love the freedom that is ours in Christ.

—Dr. Ron Phillips
Senior pastor, Abba's House
Author, *Everyone's Guide to Demons and Spiritual Warfare* and *Angels and Demons*

I have heard many teachings and read many books about Jezebel and the spirit of Jezebel. I can honestly say this is the best and most thorough teaching on the truth concerning Jezebel, her cohort, Ahab, and the spiritual army of darkness that works with her to empower her agenda of seduction. This book will help you not only see and discern when Jezebel is in operation, but also ensure there are no open doors in your personal life that will give opportunity for this evil spirit to take advantage of you. Scripture states that we are not to remain ignorant or uninformed of the schemes of the enemy, in order that he might not outwit us (2 Cor. 2:11). This book is a must-read for every believer who desires to be equipped to understand, discern, and overcome Jezebel.

—Rebecca Greenwood
Cofounder, Christian Harvest International and Strategic Prayer Action Network

Satan's hierarchy may be complex and well established, but God has given Jennifer LeClaire fascinating insight and revelation to expose the players in the devil's plot.

In *Jezebel's Puppets* she reveals the unseen battle being waged in the heavenlies by Satan and his minions against your city, church, and personal destiny. She then leads you through a riveting "tell-all" of one of the enemy's most potent principalities—Jezebel—and empowers you with practical strategies to rise up, confront, and lay waste to Satan's sham kingdom.

—Kyle Winkler
Author, *Silence Satan*
Creator, Shut Up, Devil! app

In her latest writing, *Jezebel's Puppets*, Jennifer LeClaire opens the eyes of the reader to the unseen spirit world. This book equips the church to walk free from the power of the enemy and inherit all the promises that God has provided. It is a continuation of the in-depth, original, and concise writings of one of today's premiere prophetic authors.

—Ryan LeStrange
Founder, Impact International Ministries
Cofounder, AwakeningTV.com
Author, *Releasing the Prophetic*

JEZEBEL'S PUPPETS

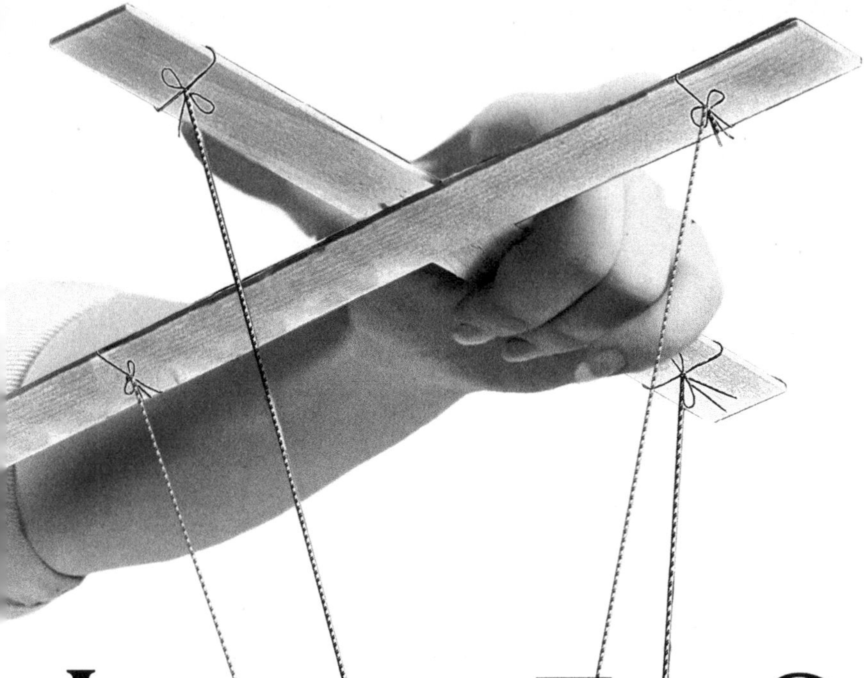

JEZEBEL'S PUPPETS

JENNIFER LECLAIRE

Most Charisma House Book Group products are available at special quantity discounts for bulk purchase for sales promotions, premiums, fund-raising, and educational needs. For details, write Charisma House Book Group, 600 Rinehart Road, Lake Mary, Florida 32746, or telephone (407) 333-0600.

Jezebel's Puppets by Jennifer LeClaire
Published by Charisma House
Charisma Media/Charisma House Book Group
600 Rinehart Road
Lake Mary, Florida 32746
www.charismahouse.com

Cover design by Justin Evans

Visit the author's website at www.jenniferleclaire.org.

Library of Congress Cataloging-in-Publication Data:
LeClaire, Jennifer (Jennifer L.)
Jezebel's puppets / Jennifer LeClaire. -- First edition.
pages cm
Includes bibliographical references.
ISBN 978-1-62998-622-7 (trade paper) -- ISBN 978-1-62998-623-4 (e-book)
1. Spiritual warfare. 2. Discernment of spirits. 3. Jezebel, Queen, consort of Ahab, King of Israel. I. Title.
BV4509.5.L4425 2014
235'.4--dc23

2015036171

While the author has made every effort to provide accurate Internet addresses at the time of publication, neither the publisher nor the author assumes any responsibility for errors or for changes that occur after publication.

First edition

16 17 18 19 20 — 987654321
Printed in the United States of America

This book is dedicated first and foremost to the principality over my life—Jesus Christ. He is the King of kings and the Lord of lords and the Prince of Peace and so much more. I magnify Him in every area of my life. He is my victory in the face of any battle. He is my wisdom in warfare. I give Him all the glory and honor for equipping those who love Him to overcome by His blood and the word of their testimony.

CONTENTS

ACKNOWLEDGMENTS

I'm grateful to Charisma House for giving me the opportunity to expose Jezebel's "puppets" to the masses with scriptural reference and practical experience. Special thanks to Joy Strang, Tessie DeVore, and Maureen Eha for encouraging me to draw out more revelation about this spirit for the body of Christ. I'm also grateful to Linda Willoughby of Keepers of the Flame and Michelle Smith for being faithful to intercede for me while writing this book.

FOREWORD

You are holding in your hand a manual, a guide—not just another book. *Jezebel's Puppets* is filled with wisdom on how to wage spiritual warfare effectively. I wish I had written this book—which is possibly one of the highest endorsements I can give. It is that thorough, that good! What a breath of fresh air. I will add some of the teaching and understanding contained in this book to my own arsenal.

As a veteran in the modern-day global prayer, prophetic, and spiritual-warfare movement, I am at times concerned with the superficiality I see in some of today's teachings, applications, and ministries—especially on subjects such as this. But when it comes to the writings of this disciple of the Lord Jesus Christ, I know I am sitting down to a steak dinner. Her teaching capacity is scripturally balanced, seasoned with historical accuracy, without fluff, and full of sound, practical applications and perspective.

Jennifer has waded into the deeper end of the pool to take on this subject matter. The term *Jezebel spirit* has been so loosely tossed around in the past that any strong woman leader who became a threat to an insecure pastor was labeled a Jezebel. And often slanderously. Now I want to be very clear with you: demonic spirits have no gender. Therefore men can be affected by and used as pawns of this demonic force as well. But this book acts as a wooden stick tossed into these muddy waters to bring healing—not accusation (Exod. 15:25).

You will read a very wise statement near the end of this encyclopedia of truth: "No one is immune to becoming a puppet in Jezebel's twisted spiritual play—not even those who preach about, pray against, and prophesy the ultimate doom of Jezebel." Again, I have to give my wholehearted, "Yes and amen!" Brilliant. That is wisdom beyond her years.

None of us are exempt, unless we walk in the light of God's Word and are cleansed by the blood of the Lamb, the Lord Jesus Christ. Pride is the downfall of many a man or woman of God. It always precedes a fall. So let's walk in the opposite spirit that Jesus taught, and let's live the Sermon on the Mount.

It is my honor and delight to endorse the teachings of Jennifer LeClaire written here—and especially the depths of wisdom and research that are contained within these pages and the prayerful approach taken in presenting this delicate subject matter. Well done! Well done indeed!

—Dr. James W. Goll
Founder, Encounters Network,
Prayer Storm, GET eSchool
International best-selling author

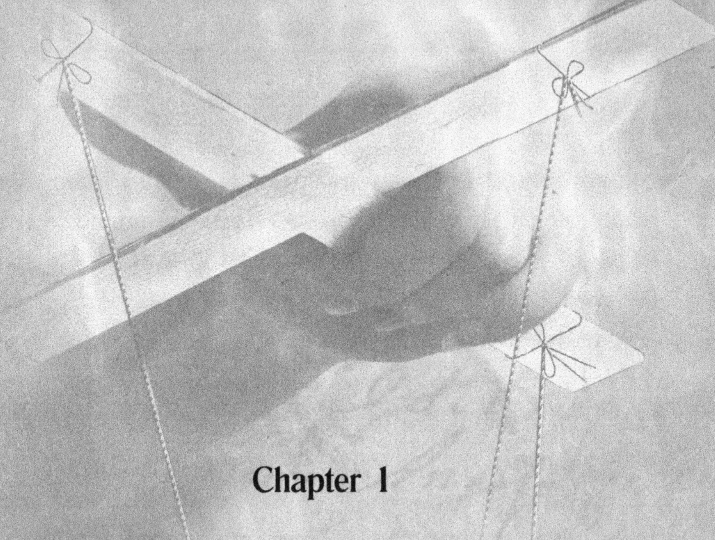

Chapter 1

SATAN'S FALLEN ANGELS

Angels are real, but I've never seen one—unless perhaps you count a fallen angel. I was camping with a friend in the Smoky Mountains in a small tent under a starless, moonless sky when I heard someone—or something—rustling around on the other side of the nylon-zippered doors. At first I thought it was just the wind blowing through the trees, but it soon became obvious that we weren't hearing merely a mountain breeze.

The next obvious conclusion was that it was some kind of animal scavenging for food. I had been warned about the bears and certainly didn't want to meet one face-to-face! But what I encountered when I peeked my head out the tent doors was nearly as scary. It was a spirit of fear.

Of course, I didn't know at the time it was a spirit of fear. All I knew was a large black mass that was darker than the starless, moonless sky lunged toward me. I barreled backward in the tent with a shrill scream that echoed into the darkness. Convinced I'd seen something—but unconvinced it was a spiritual force—my friend bravely moved toward the nylon-zippered doors to have a look-see for herself while I worked my way as far back in the tiny tent as I could get.

My friend didn't see a spirit of fear—she saw two angels in glowing white robes with swords drawn. They were standing guard over the camp. All I could hear was her saying: "Wow! Wow! Wow!" She pulled her head back into the tent and described in minute detail what she saw. I rushed forward to see this glorious sight, but there was nothing but darkness. I always joke about how unfair that was. She got to see angels, and I got to see what I later learned from wise warriors who see into the spiritual realm was a spirit of fear.

Although I saw only the opposing force—I still haven't seen an angel and don't seek to see either angels or demons—I never again doubted that spiritual warfare is real. That camping trip wasn't the last time I saw my spiritual enemies through a prophetic dream or vision, but it was the beginning of a new revelation about Satan's spiritual army, how it operates as an organized militia that opposes God's will, and how demons partner with one another at Satan's command (and sometimes go rogue) to get the devil's dirty work done.

In this chapter I'll share with you some foundational truths about Satan's kingdom that will shed light on the enemy's dark camp. Some of these scriptures may be very familiar to you, but don't gloss over them. Let the Holy Spirit take you deeper into a revelation of how your enemy operates. Let Him equip you with the truth that will set you free from the onslaught of the spirit of Jezebel and its puppets.

Satan Is Real

You can't deny the existence of Satan and his demonic clan without denying the existence of the Father, Son, Holy Spirit, and angels in heaven. The Bible speaks clearly of all these personalities whom we sense but rarely, if ever, see with our natural eyes. For example, Jesus speaks of "eternal fire, prepared for the devil and his angels" (Matt. 25:41). Jesus also said, "I saw Satan as lightning fall from heaven" (Luke 10:18). He speaks of a day when "the ruler of this world will be cast out" (John 12:31). What's more, Jesus was very clear that Satan has a kingdom that puts demon spirits to work:

> Then one possessed with a demon was brought to Him, blind and mute, and He healed him, so that the blind and mute man both spoke and saw. All the people were amazed and said, "Is He not the Son of David?" But when the Pharisees heard it, they said, "This Man does not cast out demons, except by Beelzebub the ruler of the demons." Jesus knew their thoughts and said to them, "Every kingdom divided against itself is brought to desolation. And every city or house divided against itself will not stand. If Satan casts out Satan, he is divided against himself. Then how will his kingdom stand? And if I cast out demons by Beelzebub, by whom do your sons cast them out? Therefore, they shall be your judges. But if

> I cast out demons by the Spirit of God, then the kingdom of God has come upon you.
>
> —MATTHEW 12:22–28

So let's go back to the beginning and lay a strong foundation for the reality of Satan—the enemy of our souls—and why he's our enemy. Satan wasn't always called Satan. One of God's created angels, he was once known as Lucifer—and he was full of beauty. In fact, Ezekiel 28 paints a picture of Lucifer before the fall that is beautiful and brilliant:

> You had the seal of perfection, full of wisdom and perfect in beauty. You were in Eden, the garden of God; every precious stone was your covering: the sardius, topaz, and the diamond, the beryl, the onyx, and the jasper, the sapphire, the emerald, and the carbuncle, and gold. The workmanship of your settings and sockets was in you; on the day that you were created, they were prepared. You were the anointed cherub that covers, and I set you there; you were upon the holy mountain of God; you walked up and down in the midst of the stones of fire. You were perfect in your ways from the day that you were created, until iniquity was found in you.
>
> —EZEKIEL 28:12–15

THE FALL OF LUCIFER

That passage goes on to say that Lucifer, who was an archangel like Michael, became filled with violence and sinned, forcing Father to cast him as a "profane" thing out of His presence. What was the root of his sin? Pride.

Ezekiel's prophetic chronicle tells us Lucifer's heart was lifted up because of his beauty and that his wisdom was corrupted because of his splendor (Ezek. 28:16–17). Isaiah offers more insight into the fall of Lucifer:

> How are you fallen from heaven, O Lucifer, son of the morning! How you are cut down to the ground, you who weaken the nations! For you have said in your heart, "I will ascend into heaven, I will exalt my throne above the stars of God; I will sit also on the mount of the congregation, in the recesses of the north; I will ascend above the heights of the clouds, I will be like the Most High." Yet you shall be brought down to Hell, to the sides of the pit.
>
> —Isaiah 14:12–15

But it wasn't just Lucifer who was cast out of heaven. The charismatic archangel managed to woo one-third of God's ministering spirits to his side as revealed in Revelation 12:3–4, which notes: "Then another sign appeared in heaven: There was a great red dragon with seven heads and ten horns, and seven diadems on his heads. His tail drew a third of the stars of heaven, and threw them to the earth." The dragon is none other than Satan. These verses illustrate Satan is the master of deception and knows how to tap into the pride in God's created beings, whether angelic or human.

We gain insight into the origin of the battle between good and evil from John the Apostle in the Book of Revelation:

> Then war broke out in heaven. Michael and his angels fought against the dragon, and the dragon

> and his angels fought, but they did not prevail, nor was there a place for them in heaven any longer. The great dragon was cast out, that ancient serpent called the Devil and Satan, who deceives the whole world. He was cast down to the earth, and his angels were cast down with him.
>
> —REVELATION 12:7–9

Even now Satan is warring against the saints on earth. Daniel 7:25 reveals, "He shall speak pompous words against the Most High, shall persecute the saints of the Most High, and shall intend to change times and law" (NKJV). The word *persecute* in that verse literally means to "wear out." If you've ever felt weary in well-doing, then there's a good chance that the spiritual opposition you face is what's causing you to want to give up. The enemy of your soul is relentless.

Peter warns that God resists the proud and gives grace to the humble and admonishes us to "be sober and watchful, because your adversary the devil walks around as a roaring lion, seeking whom he may devour. Resist him firmly in the faith, knowing that the same afflictions are experienced by your brotherhood throughout the world" (1 Pet. 5:8–9). Yes, the spiritual battle with Satan and wicked forces is real—and often intense—especially when you have an onslaught of demons released against you.

YOUR AUTHORITY IN CHRIST

But before we go any further, let's take a moment to remember the good news. We win! If you are born again, you have been delivered from the power of darkness (Col. 1:13). Consider the revelation John the Apostle recorded:

> Then I heard a loud voice in heaven, saying: "Now the salvation and the power and the kingdom of our God and the authority of His Christ have come, for the accuser of our brothers, who accused them before our God day and night, has been cast down. They overcame him by the blood of the Lamb and by the word of their testimony, and they loved not their lives unto the death."
>
> —Revelation 12:10–11

Yes, we win—but that doesn't mean we don't have to fight. Indeed, when we accepted Jesus as our Lord and Savior we effectively enlisted in the army of God. We're in a spiritual war whether we engage our enemy or not. If you don't understand who you are in Christ—if you don't understand your authority in Him—then you cannot successfully wage war against the enemy who is waging war against you.

There are entire volumes written on the believer's authority, but let me give you just a couple of scriptures to remind you of the power at your disposal in Jesus. First, God raised Christ from the dead by the power of the Holy Spirit and seated Him at His right hand in heavenly places, "far above all principalities, and power, and might, and dominion, and every name that is named, not only in this age but also in that which is to come. And He put all things in subjection under His feet and made Him the head over all things for the church, which is His body, the fullness of

Him who fills all things in all ways" (Eph. 1:21–23). We now are seated with Christ in heavenly places (Eph. 2:6).

Jesus gives His disciples authority over demons. We see this for the first time in Matthew 10:1: "He called His twelve disciples to Him and gave them authority over unclean spirits, to cast them out, and to heal all kinds of sickness and all kinds of disease." Before His ascension to heaven, Jesus also said, "In My name they will cast out demons; they will speak with new tongues; they will take up serpents; if they drink any deadly thing, it will not hurt them; they will lay hands on the sick, and they will recover" (Mark 16:17–18).

Our manifested victory in battle is dependent, in part, on these revelations. That's because although Jesus has already defeated the devil, we still have to enforce that victory in our own lives. If we don't understand our authority—and if we don't really know the One who has delegated His authority to us—then we can't walk in the fullness of it.

Remember the seven sons of Sceva? Some Jewish exorcists tried to cast out devils in the name of Jesus. The demons knew they weren't in relationship with Christ—the One who delegates His authority to cast out devils—and exposed them. Then the demon-possessed man prevailed against the exorcists and left them naked and wounded (Acts 19:13–17). You need a revelation both of Christ in you and you in Him to enforce His victory in your life.

When Jesus asked His disciples, "Who do you say that I am?" the Apostle Peter answered Him and said, "You are the Christ, the Son of the living God" (Matt. 16:15–16). Then Jesus answered Peter and said to him:

> Blessed are you, Simon son of Jonah, for flesh and blood has not revealed this to you, but My Father who is in heaven. And I tell you that you are Peter, and on this rock I will build My church, and the gates of Hades shall not prevail against it. I will give you the keys of the kingdom of heaven, and whatever you bind on earth shall be bound in heaven, and whatever you loose on earth shall be loosed in heaven.
>
> —MATTHEW 16:17–19

The revelation of Christ is unending. It will take an eternity to search out the depths of Christ. You don't need to be a theologian, of course, to exercise your authority in Christ over Satan and his wicked militia. But you do need to understand the power of the blood, the power of the name of Christ, and the power in your delegated authority to enforce God's will on earth just as it is in heaven. Armed with this understanding, you are ready to engage in the war in the heavens.

A DEMONIC WRESTLING MATCH

In Ephesians 6 the Apostle Paul tells us to be strong in the Lord and the power of His might—not *our* might but *His* might. Paul exhorts us to put on our spiritual armor so we can stand against the strategies of the enemy and expose the highly organized kingdom that Satan rules: "For we wrestle not against flesh and blood, but against principalities, against powers, against the rulers of the darkness of this world, against spiritual wickedness in high places" (Eph. 6:12, KJV).

In other words, the enemy may influence people to

behave a certain way, but our struggle is not ultimately with human beings. We're contending with demons working behind the scenes at various levels of authority in Satan's kingdom. Before we unpack that revelation, let's first consider the sport of wrestling. Wrestling is intense and hands-on—and you can't do it from a distance. In a high school wrestling match, for example, the competitors' bodies are often intertwined. The momentum shifts from one combatant to another until one is eventually defeated or gives up.

Spiritual warfare requires wrestling—hand-to-hand combat with bodiless enemies we can't see with our natural eyes. The Greek word for *wrestling* in Ephesians 6:12 is *palé*. The New Testament Greek Lexicon defines it as, "a contest between two in which each endeavours to throw the other, and which is decided when the victor is able to hold his opponent down with his hand upon his neck; the term is transferred to the Christian's struggle with the power of evil."[1]

Demons try to choke you—or put you in a stranglehold. In the wrestling world a stranglehold is an illegal hold that chokes the opponent. *Merriam-Webster's Dictionary* calls it a "force or influence that chokes or suppresses freedom of movement or expression."[2] If the wrestler doesn't break free from the stranglehold, the lack of blood or air can cause him to black out. Translating this to our spiritual realities, the enemy wants to choke the Word of God out of your mouth so you can't wield your sword of the Spirit or pray. The enemy wants to choke out the revelation of who you are in Christ and your authority over him.

But Satan doesn't work alone. As we see in Ephesians 6:12, Satan is head of a highly organized kingdom that depends on demons working together to get his dirty work done. Satan is the commander-in-chief, but he can't be everywhere at the same time. Therefore, he strategically recruited, enlisted, and commissioned an army of principalities, powers, rulers of the darkness of this world, and spiritual wickedness in high places to execute his wicked plans

Colossians 1:16 reveals: "For by Him all things were created that are in heaven and that are in earth, visible and invisible, whether they are thrones, or dominions, or principalities, or powers. All things were created by Him and for Him." Here we see four categories of the invisible things Christ created in order of authority: thrones, dominions, principalities, and powers. This offers additional insight into Ephesians 6:12, which starts with "principalities" and "powers" and works its way down to "spiritual wickedness in high places." Thrones and dominions were not part of Satan's rebellion. We are not wrestling against thrones and dominions.

War in the Heavens

Let's look at Ephesians 6:12 in the New King James Version of the Bible: "For we do not wrestle against flesh and blood, but against principalities, against powers, against the rulers of the darkness of this age, against spiritual hosts of wickedness in the heavenly places." Now let's key in on "heavenly places" because that's where your enemies are operating. Where are these heavenly places?

We know there's more than one heaven because in Genesis 1 the Bible says God created the "heavens" and the earth. Psalm 102:25 declares, "Of old You laid the foundation of the earth, and the heavens are the work of Your hands" (NKJV). So there's one earth, but more than one heaven. In fact, there are three heavens recorded in Scripture. Paul writes:

> I will move on to visions and revelations of the Lord. I knew a man in Christ over fourteen years ago—whether in the body or out of the body I cannot tell, God knows—such a one was caught up to the third heaven. And I knew that such a man—whether in the body or out of the body I cannot tell, God knows—was caught up into paradise and heard inexpressible words not permitted for a man to say.
>
> —2 CORINTHIANS 12:1–4

Now I am not good at math. I often joke that I'm a writer because I can't do math. But it's clear that there can't be a third heaven without a first and second heaven. This third heaven Paul writes about is obviously the location of the throne of God by virtue of the connection to "paradise." This third heaven is the highest heaven. There is no realm higher than where God sits on His throne.

So what about the first heaven and the second heaven? The first heaven is our atmosphere. Genesis 1:14 reveals, "God said, 'Let there be lights in the expanse of the heavens to separate the day from the night, and let them be signs to indicate seasons, and days, and years.'" The firmament of the heavens is the first heaven. In Deuteronomy 11:17 we see that God controls this heaven and that He can "shut up the heavens so that there will be no rain and the land will not yield its fruit, and you will quickly perish from the good land which the LORD is giving you." This is talking about our atmosphere.

The second heaven is where the stars begin. You might call this outer space. Psalm 19:1 says, "The heavens declare the glory of God, and the firmament shows His handiwork." The heavens in this verse are the stars. The sun is mentioned as part of the "heavens" in Psalm 19:4–6. And Jeremiah 8:2 talks about the sun, moon, and stars of the heavens. Again, we see three heavens in Scripture. You can dig out many other scriptures that describe each of the three heavens.

So where does the wrestling take place? This wrestling against Satan's army happens in the second heaven. Certainly there's no conflict in God's heavenly realm. Although we see conflict on the earth, it's not purely a spiritual conflict. The first and second heavens, however, do collide because principalities, powers, rulers of the darkness of this age, and spiritual hosts of wickedness in the second heaven influence people and events in the first heaven. If we wrestle effectively, then the demonic activity in the second heaven won't manifest in our lives, families, and cities.

When First and Second Heavens Collide

There are two revealing examples of this in Scripture. One is in Ezekiel 28, which mentions both a prince of Tyre and a king of Tyre. The prince of Tyre is the flesh-and-blood ruler. The king of Tyre is the spiritual ruler. The Lord prophesies against the prince of Tyre because he makes a prideful claim to be a god and promises to bring destruction to the king of Tyre's kingdom (Ezek. 28:1–10).

The Lord also prophesies to the king of Tyre. The Bible

calls him the "anointed cherub" (v. 14). Clearly this is not a person but a spirit—indeed it is Satan himself. Satan's prideful character was manifesting in the prince of Tyre, whose "heart is lifted up" and who says, "I am a god; I sit in the seat of gods in the midst of the seas" (vv. 1–2). Yet just as Satan was an angel and not a god, so the prince of Tyre is "a man, and not God, though you set your heart as the heart of God" (v. 2). Satan influenced this prince and his rulership.

We've seen this in modern days. Look at wicked world rulers such as Mussolini or Hitler. But it's not just political leaders. Look at the world of the drug trade, sex trafficking, and various other crime rings. Look at pedophilia, homosexuality, and other perversions of God's creation. Look at crimes of greed such as embezzlement or robbery. Look at racism, which is still alive and well. I'm not saying there's a devil behind every doorknob, but I am convinced there are demons in the second heaven that are influencing society through the people living in it who are not submitted to God. It's getting darker out there as the last days draw closer to an end. Devils use people to do their dirty work—but Satan is using these demons, ultimately, to do his dirty work. Again, he is the commander-in-chief of the wicked army.

The good news is we have authority. Our prayers lifted up from the first heaven impact what happens in the first and second heavens. We see this in the Book of Daniel. In Daniel 10:2 we find Daniel mourning for three weeks. He went on a fast over Israel. On the twenty-fourth day of the month God opened Daniel's eyes to the spiritual realm. He saw a man clothed in linen whose waist was wrapped with gold of Uphaz. He had a body like beryl, a face like lightning, eyes like fire, and arms like bronze, and the sound of his words were like a multitude of voices (vv. 3–6). The man said to Daniel:

> Do not be afraid, Daniel. For from the first day that you set your heart to understand this and to humble yourself before your God, your words were heard, and I have come because of your words. But the prince of the kingdom of Persia withstood me for twenty-one days. So Michael, one of the chief princes, came to help me, for I had been left there with the kings of Persia. Now I have come to make you understand what shall befall your people in the latter days. For the vision is yet for many days.
>
> —Daniel 10:12–14

You can see the conflict in the second heaven plainly in this verse. This angel got into a wrestling match with a demonic force assigned to cover Persia. This was not a natural king but one of Satan's fallen angels. This force was so strong that Michael, an archangel, came to help him overpower it. The whole skirmish in the second heaven lasted three weeks.

But after reaching Daniel with the revelations God wanted to share, the angel revealed that the battle was not yet over. He told Daniel: "Do you know why I have come to you? And now I must return to fight with the prince of Persia; and when I have gone forth, indeed the prince of Greece will come. But I will tell you what is noted in the Scripture of Truth. (No one upholds me against these, except Michael your prince. . . .)" (Dan. 10:20–21, NKJV).

We see here that Persia and Greece both have demons

assigned to them. From this we can draw the conclusion that Satan has set up princes in the second heaven over countries and cities. In my territory of South Florida the spirit of Jezebel has a strong influence. In Revelation 2:20 Jesus says, "Nevertheless I have a few things against you, because you allow that woman Jezebel, who calls herself a prophetess, to teach and seduce My servants to commit sexual immorality and eat things sacrificed to idols" (NKJV).

You can see the influence of Jezebel in South Florida—and indeed over our entire nation and even our churches—through manifestations of immorality and idolatry. According to the National Human Trafficking Resource Center, Florida ranks third for the number of reports to its antitrafficking hotline.[3] Miami Beach scores a perfect one hundred—plus eighteen bonus points—on the Human Rights Campaign's 2014 Municipal Equality Index, which measures how well cities support gay, lesbian, bisexual, and transgender people.[4] In 2008 *Forbes* magazine rated Miami the tenth most sinful city in the United States.[5] Florida has seen a number of high-profile pastors fall into sexual immorality. I could go on and on with the evidence of Jezebel's influence over the region and the state.

If Jesus Defeated Satan, Why Do We Have to Fight?

Jesus "disarmed principalities and powers, He made a public spectacle of them, triumphing over them" (Col. 2:15, NKJV). Many who oppose spiritual-warfare practices point to that scripture and say we don't have to fight because the devil is already defeated. Yes, the devil is already defeated, but after the death and resurrection of Jesus, Paul nevertheless told Timothy to "fight the good fight of faith" (1 Tim. 6:12) and told the Ephesians we "fight...against...principalities, against powers, against the rulers of the darkness of this world, and against spiritual forces of evil in the heavenly places" (Eph. 6:12).

If Satan and his demons are already defeated, why do we have to fight? Because we live in a world with Satan's fallen angels—and God's fallen men. The war is on for the souls of mankind. Competing with Jesus who sacrificed His life to set fallen man free, Satan and his demons strategize to keep God's creation in bondage through deception. The kingdom of darkness is working overtime to keep the blinders on lost souls. Part of the reason we're here is to work toward fulfilling the Great Commission:

> Jesus came and spoke to them, saying, "All authority has been given to Me in heaven and on earth. Go therefore and make disciples of all nations, baptizing them in the name of the Father and of the Son and of the Holy Spirit, teaching them to observe all things I have commanded you. And remember, I am with you always, even to the end of the age."
>
> —Matthew 28:18–20

We are Christ's ambassadors to be salt and light, to be a witness that Jesus is alive, and to preach the gospel and make disciples. Satan hates us because we are created in God's image. And so the spiritual warfare ensues. We cannot remain passive in this war. We must be good and faithful servants, fighting the good fight of faith. Jesus expects us to wrestle against principalities, against powers, against the rulers of the darkness of this world, against spiritual wickedness in high places. He expects us to co-labor with Him to set the captives free. And so the war ensues.

Paul wrote: "For though we walk in the flesh, we do not war according to the flesh. For the weapons of our warfare are not carnal, but mighty through God to the pulling down of strongholds, casting down imaginations and every high thing that exalts itself against the knowledge of God, bringing every thought into captivity to the obedience of Christ, and being ready to punish all disobedience when your obedience is complete" (2 Cor. 10:3–6).

Of course, it's not just about the lost souls. It's also about our personal relationship with God, our maturity in Christ, and fulfilling our destiny in Him. Either way, when it comes to spiritual warfare, the battle often starts in our minds. Indeed, the weapons of our warfare are not carnal but mighty in God for the pulling down of strongholds in our minds. In contrast, the weapons of Satan are carnal, mighty in our flesh for the erecting of strongholds in our minds—and we're the ones arming him. Before we can walk in fullness of power to set the captives free, we need to win the battles in our own minds. We can win those battles by casting down imaginations—which requires a revelation of the helmet of salvation—and otherwise taking up the whole armor of God. With that understanding let's look again at Ephesians 6:

> Finally, my brothers, be strong in the Lord and in the power of His might. Put on the whole armor of God that you may be able to stand against the schemes of the devil. For our fight is not against

> flesh and blood, but against principalities, against powers, against the rulers of the darkness of this world, and against spiritual forces of evil in the heavenly places.
>
> —Ephesians 6:10–12

Remember to Put Your Armor On

Thankfully Paul didn't tell us that we're in a wrestling match with enemies who seek to put us in a stranglehold without being equipped with practical solutions for battle. He followed that thought with a specific instruction:

> Stand therefore, having your waist girded with truth, having put on the breastplate of righteousness, having your feet fitted with the readiness of the gospel of peace, and above all, taking the shield of faith, with which you will be able to extinguish all the fiery arrows of the evil one. Take the helmet of salvation and the sword of the Spirit, which is the word of God. Pray in the Spirit always with all kinds of prayer and supplication. To that end be alert with all perseverance and supplication for all the saints.
>
> —Ephesians 6:14–18

When discussing the whole armor of God, the first line of defense is the truth. When you know the truth, you won't fall for the enemy's lies. The problem is, many sit in churches and hear the truth for years and years (and years) but are still quick to give ear to the enemy's lies. They are, as Paul wrote, "always learning, but never able to come to the knowledge of the truth" (2 Tim. 3:7). When you aren't a student of the Word—when you aren't a doer of the Word—the devil doesn't have to work too hard. As James said, "Be doers of the word and not hearers only, deceiving yourselves" (James 1:22). By the same token, if you don't understand the reality of the warfare against you, you won't rightly battle.

As we discussed earlier, you need a revelation of who you are in Christ. This is how you fortify your breastplate of righteousness. Understand this: "God made Him who knew no sin to be sin for us, that we might become the righteousness of God in Him" (2 Cor. 5:21). Our righteousness comes through faith in Jesus Christ (Rom. 3:22). We need to keep our shield of faith lifted high, knowing that God is trustworthy and His Word never fails. Then when the enemy launches his fiery darts, the water of the Word will extinguish the flames before they set our thoughts ablaze. The helmet of salvation—understanding what belongs to each of us as a born-again believer—will help protect our thoughts.

One of the biggest areas in which we miss it is with our mouths. Out of the abundance of the heart the mouth speaks (Luke 6:45), so we need to work with God to purify our hearts and find deliverance from corrupting forces. Paul instructs us to take the sword of the Spirit, which is the Word of God (Eph. 6:17). When we speak the Word of God out of our mouths, it serves as a weapon that cuts through every evil plot of the enemy. No devil in hell can come against the Word of God because it's not carnal but mighty—supernatural—in God.

When we find ourselves in the midst of the battle, though, we too often make one of these three common mistakes: (1) We fail to wield the sword of the Spirit, which is the Word of God; (2) we speak the enemy's fearful lies out of our mouths; or (3) we are double-minded, speaking the Word of God one moment and the enemy's fear-laced lies the next. The only sure way to enforce Jesus's victory in our lives is to consistently wield the sword of the Spirit.

Enforcing Christ's Victory

Let's look at each option and how it works. First, when we wield the sword of the Spirit, we are packing a powerful weapon. The writer of Hebrews says, "For the word of God is alive, and active, and sharper than any two-edged sword, piercing even to the division of soul and spirit, of joints and marrow, and able to judge the thoughts and intents of the heart" (Heb. 4:12).

The sword of the Spirit is sharper than any natural sword. It has supernatural power, but we have to speak out the living power it contains with our tongues. Inspired by the life-giving Holy Spirit, the wisest man on the earth once wrote, "Death and life are in the power of the tongue" (Prov. 18:21).

Our words are weapons. When we speak God's Word out of our mouths, it casts out death and opens the door to life in our situations. When we make the mistake of speaking the enemy's fearful lies out of our mouths—which may sound like worry, doubt, unbelief, or something other than the pure truth—we are allowing the enemy to use our own words as weapons against us.

Again, the devil's weapons are carnal in the sense that he works through our carnal nature to oppress us by successfully tempting us to speak death with our powerful tongues. We essentially arm the enemy with weapons of death and give him ammunition to oppress us when we speak words that are out of alignment with God's truth.

When we are double-minded, speaking the Word of God one moment and the enemy's fearful lies the next, we allow the enemy to take ground in our lives. Have you ever felt as if you were taking one step forward and two steps back? This is often the result of double-mindedness. We speak life out of our mouths, penetrating the enemy's plans with the sword of the Spirit in the morning, but as soon as we see a circumstance that doesn't go our way, we once again arm the enemy with carnal weapons through our words.

The Bible says a double-minded man is unstable in all his ways (James 1:8). If you are feeling unstable, as if the enemy is tossing you around a wrestling ring and about to capture you in a figure-four hold, it may be because you are not speaking words of faith and life—you may be arming the enemy with words of fear, doubt, unbelief, and death.

Now that you are equipped with an understanding of Satan and his fallen angels—and have a general understanding of spiritual-warfare principles that many other books expound upon in great detail—we are ready to expose Jezebel's kingdom of darkness.

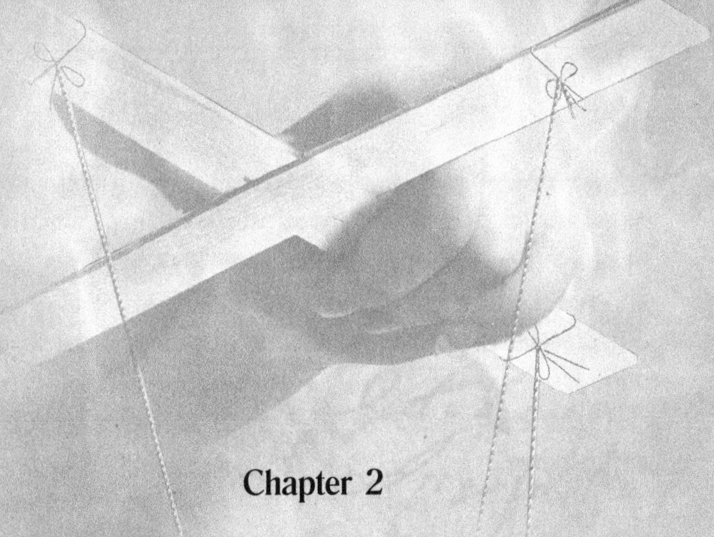

Chapter 2

PULLING THE MASK OFF JEZEBEL'S PUPPETS

As a young girl I broke my right leg twice—once skateboarding and once playing ball. Those serious fractures left me bedridden in a body cast for the better part of two years. During that time there wasn't much I could do except draw, read books, or watch television. There was no Nintendo, no PlayStation, no Xbox 360—there wasn't even an Atari with Space Invaders and Pac-Man yet. In fact, cable television was still a distant dream. My viewing choices were mostly black-and-white reruns of 1960s TV shows in the mornings and soap operas, game shows, and cartoons in the afternoons.

One show I found especially intriguing was *To Tell the Truth*. It featured four celebrities who asked questions of three people who claimed they had some unique experience or strange occupation. All three people stood in front of the celebrities and confidently stated: "My name is Mr. Brown" (or whatever the true central character's name was). Of course, they all weren't Mr. Brown. Two of the three were imposters. The two imposters were allowed to answer the panel's questions with flat-out lies, but the real Mr. Brown had to tell the truth, the whole truth, and nothing but the truth.

After asking a series of questions, the celebrities had to decide who they thought was telling the truth. They made their guesses, and then the moment of truth came when the host asked, "Will the real Mr. Brown please stand up?" Often one of the imposters, then the other, would begin to stand up to claim they were Mr. Brown. Finally, the real Mr. Brown revealed himself, sometimes to the shock and dismay of the panel. *To Tell the Truth* was a game of deception that illustrated how difficult it is for people to determine who is telling the truth and who is lying.

It's the same in the spirit world. Without the Holy Spirit's discernment, you are merely playing a spiritual game of *To Tell the Truth* with the Jezebel spirit and its cronies. I am convinced that far too many people are going to war against Jezebel when it's not Jezebel that's harassing them. I am convinced that far too many people are calling out Jezebel in their churches or workplaces when it's not Jezebel at all.

Make no mistake, Jezebel ranks high in the kingdom of darkness, but Jezebel isn't boasting about it. This spirit flows in the realm of subtle seduction and deadly deception—and it's not going to tell the truth about what it really is. In other words, asking, "Will the real Jezebel please stand up?" isn't going to get you far in your personal battle against this enemy. Jezebel is a master of disguise, often hiding behind other spirits to protect itself and forward its agenda. I call these other spirits "Jezebel's puppets." You might not always see Jezebel, but this spirit is like a puppet master who pulls the strings behind the scenes. In this demonic puppet show Jezebel is in complete control.

Of course, that doesn't mean Jezebel's puppets aren't dangerous in their own right. We'll look more closely at each puppet and at how to cut ties with these wicked spirits in later chapters. For now I want to paint a picture for you. I want to pull back a curtain so you can see into the spiritual realm and know what's really going on behind the scenes. After you connect the dots between the spirit of Jezebel and its puppets, you'll begin to see clearly why your warfare against Jezebel sometimes seems ineffective.

Will the Real Jezebel Please Stand Up?

Again, the spirit of Jezebel isn't in the habit of making itself known—and the many books and articles with incomplete revelation about this sinister spirit can often confuse matters for young spiritual warriors seeking to enforce Christ's victory. Be careful not to put much stock in Internet checklists that claim to unmask Jezebel or you could wind up unleashing unnecessary warfare against yourself by engaging in the wrong battle.

I speak from experience. Although no one has the complete revelation of what the spirit of Jezebel is and how it operates, we'd do well to stick with what the Bible says and pepper in some personal warfare experience than to depend on Google's millions of answers to the question: "What is the spirit of Jezebel?" The truth is, there are not five ways to stop the Jezebel spirit overnight. Anyone who markets in that manner is merely merchandising the saints.

So what is the spirit of Jezebel? I'll give you one important nugget of truth: it's not the spirit of control. Although the Jezebel spirit seeks to control people—including its puppets—Jezebel and the spirit of control are two different demons. The spirit of Jezebel is a seducing spirit that wants to tempt you into sin and turn you away from God. We'll look more closely at this in a minute. First, I will establish where Jezebel sits in the kingdom of darkness.

Although we call Jezebel "the spirit of Jezebel," it's actually a principality. Ephesians 6:12 speaks to the hierarchy of demons in Satan's kingdom: "For our fight is not against flesh and blood, but against principalities, against powers, against the rulers of the darkness of this world, and against spiritual forces of evil in the heavenly places."

I believe Jezebel sits at the top of the hierarchy—not alone but with other principalities. As such, it stands to reason that Jezebel would have powers, rulers of the darkness of this age, and spiritual hosts of wickedness in heavenly places at its disposal. Just as the person Jezebel in the Old Testament was a queen who carried a measure of authority in the kingdom of Israel—and the person Jezebel in the Book of Revelation had a measure of authority in the church—the spirit of Jezebel could be likened to a general in Satan's army that has a measure of authority in the kingdom of darkness.

Some people won't admit there is such a thing as a

Jezebel spirit even though it's evident that both Queen Jezebel in 1 Kings and the false prophetess Jezebel in Revelation 2 carry the same fundamental characteristics that led people into immorality and idolatry. I believe denying the existence of Jezebel is one reason this spirit continues to take out our pastors and set up believers to blend idolatrous religions into Christianity in the name of tolerance. Some who reject the reality of the spirit of Jezebel are flowing in a natural mind, a place that will never discern the real Jezebel.

Paul said it best: "But the natural, nonspiritual man does not accept or welcome or admit into his heart the gifts and teachings and revelations of the Spirit of God, for they are folly (meaningless nonsense) to him; and he is incapable of knowing them [of progressively recognizing, understanding, and becoming better acquainted with them] because they are spiritually discerned and estimated and appreciated. But the spiritual man tries all things [he examines, investigates, inquires into, questions, and discerns all things]" (1 Cor. 2:14–15, AMPC).

The revelation that there is, indeed, a Jezebel spirit is reasonable to the natural mind and is nonsense to many Christians who truly love Jesus with all their hearts. But I assure you, the Jezebel spirit is real and is spiritually discerned. So set your heart now to examine, investigate, inquire into, and question Jezebel and its puppets lest you fall prey to this unseen enemy.

A Sinister Spirit of Seduction

This bears repeating: the spirit of Jezebel got its name from the characteristics Queen Jezebel in the Old

Testament and the woman Jezebel in the New Testament manifested. It's unlikely that God refers to this principality as "the spirit of Jezebel"; rather, that is a name Christians have devised to describe it. The Jezebel spirit, in reality, is a spirit of seduction that manifests as a false teacher and false prophetess. You can see this in the Book of Revelation in a letter to what the New King James Version of the Bible calls "the corrupt church" in Revelation 2:18–29:

> And to the angel of the church in Thyatira write, "These things says the Son of God, who has eyes like a flame of fire, and His feet like fine brass: 'I know your works, love, service, faith, and your patience; and as for your works, the last are more than the first. Nevertheless I have a few things against you, because you allow that woman Jezebel, who calls herself a prophetess, to teach and seduce My servants to commit sexual immorality and eat things sacrificed to idols. And I gave her time to repent of her sexual immorality, and she did not repent. Indeed I will cast her into a sickbed, and those who commit adultery with her into great tribulation, unless they repent of their deeds. I will kill her children with death, and all the churches shall know that I am He who searches the minds and hearts. And I will give to each one of you according to your works. Now to you I say, and to the rest in Thyatira, as many as do not have this doctrine, who have not known the depths of Satan, as they say, I will put on you no other burden. But hold fast what you have till I come. And he who overcomes, and keeps My works until the end, to

> him I will give power over the nations—"He shall rule them with a rod of iron; they shall be dashed to pieces like the potter's vessels"—as I also have received from My Father; and I will give him the morning star. He who has an ear, let him hear what the Spirit says to the churches.'"

Can you see it? Jesus charged this woman with seducing His servants. We'll dig deeper into this agenda in the next chapter, but I want you to see that the spirit of Jezebel is not merely about control. We can go back to Queen Jezebel and see this spirit of seduction working in the same way. We know that Ahab married Jezebel, and she almost immediately seduced him away from serving Jehovah, and Jehovah alone, to serving and worshipping Baal (1 Kings 16:31). Your first step toward victory against Jezebel is to see what this spirit really is. As long as you are fighting against control and think it's Jezebel, you won't find spiritual relief from the demonic pressure.

The Unassuming Ahab Spirit

Now that you see Jezebel is more than what you may have once thought, let's look at the spirit of Ahab. Again, we refer to this demon as "Ahab" in spiritual-warfare circles because the wicked king personified many of the anti-God characteristics of this spirit. Ahab is one of Jezebel's puppets.

Let's start by looking at Ahab, the natural man influenced by a demon spirit. It's not clear exactly when Ahab gave himself over to the demons that we'll explore more in depth in a later chapter. But it seems rebellion opened the door to the demonic in his life, as is often the case. Rebellion is not the only thing that opens us up to demons, but rebellion will always put you in danger of inviting a demon spirit to fortify an anti-God stance.

Ahab was the son of King Omri. Ahab ruled over the northern ten tribes of Israel, was the seventh king of the northern kingdom, and reigned for twenty-two years. He was ruler over much. According to *Encyclopedia Britannica*, his empire spanned the territory east of the Jordan River, in Gilead and probably Bashan, and into the land of Moab.[1] This made him one of the most powerful men on the earth in his day. Although it has been said that absolute power corrupts absolutely, it may not have been power that actually corrupted Ahab. In this case it was the fear of losing that power that motivated Ahab to take many of the corrupt actions that God hated.

Indeed, Ahab was an astute politician and was motivated by preserving and expanding his political power. For example, he didn't fall in love with Jezebel, sweep her off her feet, and make her queen in some grand romance. Theirs was not a Ruth and Boaz love story gone bad. Ahab married Jezebel to establish a political alliance with the Phoenicians. Jezebel was the daughter of Ethbaal of Sidon, the king of Tyre, an area also known as Phoenicia. Ethbaal was a strong politician in his own right, expanding his political power far and wide.

Ahab: The Mighty and Rebellious Warrior

Doubtless Jezebel was raised in a household where power was celebrated and war was propagated. By marrying Ahab, Jezebel attained a measure of power in her own right. For his part, Ahab forged close ties with a successful politician to advance his kingdom. But the union likely offended God even before Ahab started worshipping Jezebel's false gods. God saw the idolatry coming and warned the Israelites hundreds of years earlier before they entered the Promised Land:

> You shall not intermarry with them. You shall not give your daughters to their sons or take their daughters for your sons. For they will turn your sons away from following Me to serve other gods. Then the anger of the Lord will be inflamed against you, and He will quickly destroy you. But this is how you shall deal with them: You shall destroy their altars and break down their images and cut down their Asherim and burn their graven images with fire. For you are a holy people to the Lord your God. The Lord your God has chosen you to be His special people, treasured above all peoples who are on the face of the earth.
>
> —Deuteronomy 7:3–6

Indeed, one of the first things we learn about Ahab is that he seemed dead set on rebellion. Deuteronomy 17:18–20 commands the kings of Israel:

> When he sits on the throne of his kingdom, that he shall write a copy of this law for himself on a scroll before the priests, the Levites. It must be with him, and he must read it all the days of his life so that he may learn to fear the LORD his God, and carefully observe all the words of this law and these statutes, and do them, that his heart will not be lifted up above his brothers and so that he may not turn aside from the commandment, to the right or to the left, to the end, so that he may prolong his days in his kingdom, he and his children, in the midst of Israel.

It's not clear if Ahab obeyed this command to write himself a copy of the laws, but based on what Scripture records, it's clear that even if he did write them—and read them—he didn't obey them. If he had he wouldn't have married Jezebel in the first place. Nevertheless, the Bible says, "The sins of Jeroboam the son of Nebat were seen as minor for him to walk in, for he took Jezebel the daughter of Ethbaal, king of the Sidonians, as his wife and went and served Baal and worshipped him" (1 Kings 16:31).

Although we know Jezebel manipulated Ahab, he wasn't cowardly and weak. Ahab was mighty in battle, an aspect of his character that is often overshadowed by his association with his warring wife. He went to war three times against Ben-Hadad, the king of Syria. In fact, Ben-Hadad once gathered thirty-two kings to besiege Samaria before sending a message to Ahab that his kingdom was next (1 Kings 20:1–3). Ahab defied him, engaged him in battle, and ultimately defeated him. The encounter ended with Ben-Hadad begging Ahab to spare his life. For all his might in battle, though, Jezebel pulled the strings of his power behind the scenes.

Jezebel's False Prophets

The Jezebel spirit utters demonic prophetic words—fearful and controlling curses—that seek to put the righteous in bondage. The Bible says that Jezebel massacred the prophets of the Lord (1 Kings 18:4). It was more than the true prophetic voice she was trying to kill. I believe Jezebel was trying to do away with the one true God so that her false gods could reign supreme. With Ahab's blessing, Jezebel worked to lead Israel into idolatry, setting up her false gods and false prophets.

Obadiah, who was in charge of Ahab's house—a man the Bible says greatly feared the Lord—gathered one hundred prophets and hid them in caves. Obadiah faithfully delivered bread and water to the caves to sustain these true prophetic voices (v. 4). This was no small feat in the days of drought. Jezebel's false prophets, meanwhile, were eating at the wicked queen's table as if there were no tomorrow (and no drought). Jezebel had 850 prophets in her pocket—450 prophets of Baal and 400 prophets of Asherah—and she used them to help her forward her wicked agenda.

I believe Elijah's defeat of Jezebel's false prophets at Mount Carmel was the beginning of the end of Ahab's kingdom. Israel got a glimpse of the true prophetic and the impotence of the false prophetic and decided to turn back to the Lord, at least temporarily. As the story goes, Elijah told Ahab to gather Israel and Jezebel's prophets at Mount Carmel. Ahab complied, and Elijah asked a pointed question: "How long will you falter between two opinions? If the Lord is God, follow Him; but if Baal, follow him" (1 Kings 18:21, NKJV). The Israelites were not yet ready to make a commitment. The Bible says, "The people answered him not a word" (v. 21, NKJV).

Elijah set the stage for the showdown. He and the false prophets each got one bull, cut it into pieces, and laid it on wood without any fire under it. Each would call on the name of their god, and the god who consumed the offering with fire would stand as the one true God (vv. 23–34). Both sides were equally confident—both the true prophet and the false prophets were bold as lions. The only problem was, the united cry of Jezebel's 850 false prophets—combined with their leaping around the altar and self-mutilation from morning until evening—did not yield fire from heaven (vv. 26–29).

As the sun was setting, the false prophets were surely worn out and frustrated. Even they were probably beginning to doubt the reality of the false gods to which they had given their lives. That's when Elijah stepped in, soaked his altar and his sacrifice with water three times—filling the trench with water—and cried out to the Lord God of Abraham, Isaac, and Israel:

> At the time of the offering of the evening sacrifice, Elijah the prophet came near and said, "The Lord, God of Abraham, Isaac, and of Israel, let it be known this day that You are God in Israel and that I am Your servant and that I have done all these things at Your word. Hear me, O Lord, hear me, so that this people may know that You are the

> LORD God and that You have turned their hearts back again." Then the fire of the LORD fell and consumed the burnt sacrifice and the wood and the stones and the dust and licked up the water that was in the trench. When all the people saw it, they fell on their faces and said, "The LORD, He is God! The LORD, He is God!"
>
> —1 KINGS 18:36–39

Elijah told them to seize the false prophets, and they were executed at the Kishon brook. At that point even if Jezebel raised up another company of false prophets—and we know Jezebel and Ahab did gather another band of idolatrous yes-men to prophesy smooth sayings to them—Israel's eyes were now opened. The drought ended, and God was glorified. Although Ahab and Jezebel were still king and queen of the kingdom, the battle at Mount Carmel foreshadowed Jezebel's own demise. In order to take down Jezebel, it's necessary to cast down the false prophetic voices this spirit uses to intimidate you.

JEZEBEL'S EUNUCHS

The infrastructure of Jezebel's false kingdom also relies on eunuchs. The dictionary definition of a eunuch is a man who has been castrated, usually before puberty. In Bible times eunuchs were used to guard women's living areas. Because they were castrated, they would have no sexual desire for a woman. Eunuchs, for example, helped prepare Esther and other women to meet King Ahasuerus as he searched for a new wife (Esther 2:15).

When Jesus taught on celibacy, He said, "For there are some eunuchs who have been so from birth, there are some eunuchs who have been made eunuchs by men, and there are some eunuchs who have made themselves eunuchs for the sake of the kingdom of heaven. He who is able to receive this, let him receive it" (Matt. 19:12–13).

Jesus gave dignity to eunuchs who made themselves eunuchs for the kingdom of heaven's sake. He's speaking here, though, of men who decide not to get married for kingdom reasons rather than one born as a eunuch or one made to become a eunuch against his will. Eunuchs were not held in high regard in Bible days. Leviticus 21:21 says: "No man who has a blemish from the offspring of Aaron the priest shall come near to offer the food offerings of the LORD made by fire. He has a blemish; he shall not come near to offer the bread of his God." The list of defects includes eunuchs.

However, eunuchs were not cut off from the covenant with God. "For thus says the LORD: 'To the eunuchs who keep My Sabbaths, and choose the things that please Me, and take hold of My covenant, to them I will give in My house and within My walls a memorial, and a name better than that of sons and of daughters; I will give them an everlasting name that shall not be cut off" (Isa. 56:4–5).

We'll talk more about eunuchs in a later chapter. The point I want to make now is that Queen Jezebel took advantage of the eunuchs, who were servants in Ahab's house, to get her dirty work done. As eunuchs, these servants were expected to do the bidding of their masters. Since society held eunuchs in low esteem, they could be removed easily or even killed for disobedience. As such, eunuchs were typically faithful to perform their duties—though not always truly loyal to their masters. Jezebel surely took advantage of her high position—and their low position—in society to handle tasks that helped her forward her evil plots. They were powerless to rise up against her—until Jehu arrived on the scene. This same dynamic holds true in the spirit realm today.

Jezebel's Offspring

Ahab and Jezebel had many children. The Bible describes three of them in some detail: Athaliah, Ahaziah, and Jehoram. A Scripture study reveals Jezebel's evil influence on their lives. We'll explore these figures in a later chapter, but let's take a quick look at each.

According to *Smith's Bible Dictionary*, the name *Athaliah* means "afflicted of the Lord," and *Easton's Bible Dictionary* defines the name as "whom God afflicts."[2] That seems like a fitting name for a daughter of this wicked queen. With parents who sought political alliances to advance their kingdom, Athaliah was given in marriage to Jehoram, the eldest son of Judah's King Jehoshaphat (2 Kings 8:18). Jehoshaphat would probably rethink that marriage if he had it to do over again. Athaliah actually murdered her own grandchildren to gain power (2 Chron. 22:10), outdoing the evil of her wicked mother.

Another of Jezebel's offspring was Ahaziah. His name means "held by Jehovah," according to *Easton's Bible Dictionary*.[3] But his good name did not produce good character. He took after Ahab but was clearly influenced by his evil mother—Jezebel taught him to worship Baal and Ashtoreth. Ahaziah was the eighth king of Israel, succeeding Ahab after he was killed in battle. But he learned nothing from his parents' demise. He consulted with false gods for counsel when he was sick instead of turning his heart to God, another manifestation of the false prophetic connected to Jezebel. (See 2 Kings 1:2.)

Finally, Jehoram was Ahaziah's brother. He was king of the northern kingdom of Israel and ruled twelve years (2 Kings 3:1). Although *Smith's Bible Dictionary* defines his name as "whom Jehovah has exalted" and *Hitchcock's Bible Names Dictionary* defines Jehoram as "exaltation of the Lord," he did not live up to his name.[4] Indeed, Jezebel taught him to worship Baal, and he practiced idolatry. At one point the prophet Elisha tried to help Jehoram by revealing Syria's battle plans, but he later turned on the man of God and actually vowed to kill him, just as Jezebel wanted to kill Elijah (2 Kings 6:31). Like mother, like son.

The lesson here is that we need to be cautious not only of Jezebel but also of Jezebel's children—or in our day Jezebel's spiritual children. Christians who sit under a ministry where Jezebel rules can take on the characteristics of Jezebel even if they aren't flowing in a full-blown Jezebel spirit. You'll understand where all these puppets fit in better in the next chapter, where I start to unfold Jezebel's master plot.

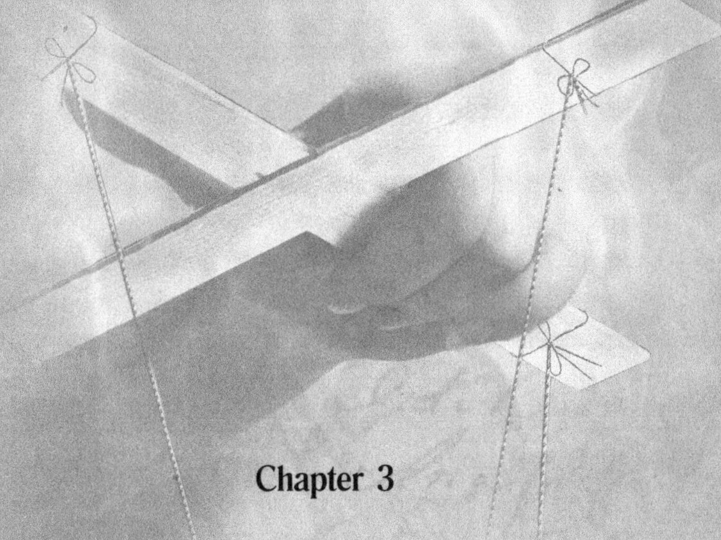

Chapter 3

JEZEBEL'S MASTER PLOT

LONG BEFORE I became a writer, I wanted to be a filmmaker. Week after week during my college years I sat in the cinema and imagined seeing my name in the credits at the end of the film. I rarely go to the movies anymore, but I still appreciate cinematic art from the likes of Swedish director, writer, and producer Ingmar Bergman, and enjoy plots in classic films such as *Casablanca* from the comfort of my home.

One classic movie that I didn't particularly enjoy was *Jezebel*, a 1938 movie starring Bette Davis and Henry Fonda. Set in 1852 New Orleans, the romantic drama follows Julie Marsden, a strong-willed Southern woman who likes to control her fiancé, a successful banker. Julie, who the movie suggests typifies the biblical Jezebel, stirs up plenty of trouble, including death, and capitalizes off a yellow-fever epidemic.

The acting is brilliant. The writing is strong. The

directing is solid. But I don't like this classic movie for one reason: it propagates misunderstandings of the spirit of Jezebel. No, I don't expect that modern Christians are taking their cues from the plot of this 1938 movie, but many of the concepts in the film have worked their way into the twenty-first century mind-set of how the Jezebel spirit operates. Those concepts only scratch the surface of Jezebel's true testimony—and leave the twists and turns of this principality's master plot hidden from the masses.

In chapter 2 I gave you a quick look at Jezebel's supporting cast. Now it's time to look at the main character—the spirit of Jezebel—and the master plot of this principality that impacted nations long before anyone attempted to name it after a queen. In other words, the spirit of Jezebel has been forwarding its end-times agenda before chroniclers recorded Queen Jezebel's story. This ancient plot, though, is drawing to its climax, and many are still ignorant of this demon's devices (2 Cor. 2:11). What, then, is Jezebel's master plot?

Jezebel's Master Plot

I recently decided to rekindle my dream to write screenplays, and it got me thinking: If I were writing the script for a movie about the spirit of Jezebel, how would the plot summary read? What would be the story line? Before I share my creative exposé, I'll show you what a plot summary looks like.

Take the plot summary for *Grace Unplugged* as an example. From the film's website: "Having just turned 18, Grace Trey aspires to more than just singing at her church, where the worship leader is her father—a former pop star. So, with the help of Mossy, her dad's former manager, Grace records a cover version of her dad's old Top-10 hit, runs off to Los Angeles, and begins to taste the kind of stardom she's always dreamed about. Yet with each rung of the ladder she climbs, Grace feels more and more pressure to compromise her values, further straining her relationship with her parents. Will everything she experiences lead her to reject her faith…or rediscover it?"[1]

Here's my plot summary for Jezebel: "A wicked spirit that has roamed the earth for thousands of years seeking someone to entice into sin, Jezebel is more than the spirit of control and manipulation that many make it out to be. Jezebel is a spirit of seduction that works to woo people into immorality and idolatry—but it doesn't work alone. With the help of Ahab, false prophets, and faithful servants, Jezebel has been sinking its seductive teeth into society for ages—and has infiltrated the pulpit and the pews of the church. Since few see Jezebel for what it is, this spirit continues to seduce the hearts and minds of those who claim Jesus as their first and true love. Will Jezebel ultimately lead the church into a great falling away or will the church wake up to this perversion before it's too late?"

That's what I call Jezebel's "master plot." But Jesus said it better in the Book of Revelation. Yes, this Jesus who has eyes like a flame of fire and feet like fine brass addressed the operation of this spirit in the end-times church. Keep in mind that He wasn't calling the church in which Jezebel was freely operating altogether wicked. Indeed, the church was doing many good things in its community. Nevertheless, doing good works doesn't make up for tolerating sin in the eyes of our Savior. Let's read what Jesus told the angel of the church in Thyatira to write:

> I know your works, love, service, faith, and your patience, and that your last works are more than the first. But I have a few things against you: You permit that woman Jezebel, who calls herself a prophetess, to teach and seduce My servants to commit sexual immorality and eat food sacrificed to idols.
>
> —REVELATION 2:19–20

That is the Jezebel spirit's agenda—and it's especially wicked—but that isn't the whole story. This slice of Scripture offers us a glimpse at the antagonist's motivation. Jezebel's goal is to seduce God's people—and not just God's people, as Jezebel is thrilled to hold anyone in bondage. So again, the motivation is clear, but the endgame is not. We have to dive deeper into Scripture to find out where Jezebel ultimately wants to lead you.

Jesus made a clear contrast between His purpose and the devil's purpose, and John recorded it in his gospel, revealing, "The thief does not come, except to steal and kill and destroy. I came that they may have life, and that they may have it more abundantly" (John 10:10). Make no mistake, the spirit of Jezebel is a thief. The difference with Jezebel is how it works: Jezebel does more than tempt you. Jezebel seduces you into two specific areas: immorality and idolatry.

Immorality in the Pulpit and the Pews

Doubtless you've witnessed the demolishing power of immorality. Allegations of immorality rocked the White House when President Bill Clinton insisted he did not have sex with then-twenty-two-year-old intern Monica Lewinsky—only later to admit his "inappropriate relationship."[2] He's not the first government official to fall into sexual immorality, nor the first business leader, nor the first pastor, nor the first parishioner.

As part of my editorial role at *Charisma* magazine, I've had the great displeasure of reporting on fallen pastor after fallen pastor after fallen pastor. I hate covering these stories. The redeeming value in our coverage is offering hope, encouraging prayer, and allowing strong Christian voices to become voices of reason in the midst of a tragic situation. If we don't cover it, the secular media merely has a field day with it, sometimes nearly celebrating the fall of a popular Christian persona. But I still don't like that it happens.

After three pastors fell into sexual immorality during a six-month period in Orlando, I prayerfully investigated the issue. If those were the only three pastors to rock their churches with sex scandals, it would be hurtful enough. But sexual immorality and idolatry are growing trends in the church—and I imagine they're more prevalent in the pews than they are in the pulpits. The spirit of Jezebel is often behind this immoral trend, tapping in to the lust of the flesh with its seductive agenda.

Sadly the spirit of Jezebel is picking off pastors one by one as they succumb to the evil desires in their own hearts. No, I'm not picking on pastors. As I said, parishioners are also falling into the same trap I'm about to expose—and none of us are immune to Jezebel's seductions. Jeremiah prophesied this, "The heart is more deceitful than all things and desperately wicked; who can understand it?" (Jer. 17:9). If we think there's no way we could ever possibly fall for Jezebel's deception then we're already deceived.

I assure you that no God-fearing believer takes immorality—or enters into it—quickly or lightly. The Jezebel spirit is patient in its seduction, often using its puppets to help set the stage for your fall. The problem, even in some spiritual-warfare circles, is that too few recognize the sinister workings of Jezebel's stealth seduction. They are either tolerating sexual immorality in the church or merely failing to recognize the true Jezebel in operation because they are on a witch hunt for controlling, manipulative women.

So before we look at the demolishing power of immorality, let's take a closer look at how the Jezebel spirit works in this realm. Again, Jezebel is essentially a spirit of seduction that woos people into sexual immorality and idolatry. Jezebel comes to kill, steal, and destroy by tempting you and then escorting you, willingly, into immorality and idolatry.

Christ's words bear repeating because you really need to catch what Jesus said about Jezebel's master plot. Again, Jesus said, "I know your works, love, service, faith, and your patience, and that your last works are more than the first. But I have a few things against you: You permit that woman Jezebel, who calls herself a prophetess, to teach and seduce My servants to commit sexual immorality and eat food sacrificed to idols" (Rev. 2:19–20). We have a responsibility to resist the devil and he will flee. Jezebel is no exception, but many continue falling because they don't see the big picture—some refuse to acknowledge there is a spirit of Jezebel. Meanwhile, Jezebel justifies the sins of immorality and idolatry with a false doctrine of grace.

The Defiling Power of Immorality

Immorality can be deadly—and Jezebel knows this. That's why seducing you into immorality is part of this spirit's master plot. If you study what the Bible says about immorality, it's sobering. Indeed, a serious study on the defiling power of immorality will put the fear of God in your heart. So let's take a moment right now to study this out. As you read this, I pray the Spirit of the fear of the Lord described in Isaiah 11:2 will pour over you because embracing the Spirit of the fear of the Lord is one safeguard against falling prey to the Jezebel spirit.

First, I want to be clear that we can't blame Jezebel if we fall into immorality. Jezebel is merely the seducer. We have a free will, and we don't have to give in to this seduction. Jezebel's captives never go kicking and screaming. Paul clearly lists fornication and adultery (two manifestations of immorality) as a work of the flesh (Gal. 5:19). Again, Jezebel can't force you into immorality. You have to choose to cooperate with this defiling spirit.

God has been warning about the dangers of immorality since Leviticus, which outlines various laws. Reading Leviticus 18 makes it clear that God stands against immorality because of its defiling power. God outlines various forms of sexual immorality, which include sexual relations with relatives, sexual relations with one of the same sex, and sexual relations with animals. We see all these perversions rising in these last days. If you type keywords such as *bestiality* and *incest* into Google News, you'll get a long list of stories.

God says in Leviticus 18:24–29: "Do not defile yourselves in any of these ways, for in these practices the nations I am casting out before you have defiled themselves. And the land has become defiled; therefore I have punished its iniquity, and the land has vomited out her inhabitants. But you shall therefore keep My statutes and My decrees, and you shall not commit any of these abominations, either the native citizen or any foreigner who sojourns among you (for the people of the land, who were before you, committed all of these abominations, and the land became defiled), lest the land vomit you out also when you defile it, as it vomited out the nations that were before you. For whoever shall commit any of these abominations, those persons who commit them shall be cut off from among their people."

Strong words. Of course, we're in an age of grace. Jesus Christ came to pay the price for our sins. We can repent of immorality, receive God's forgiveness, and start fighting the good fight of faith again. But when we wallow in immorality, it defiles us. The word *defile* in that scripture is from the Hebrew root "tame," which suggests something that is unclean, impure, polluted, or contaminated. First and foremost, immorality hinders our relationship with God.

Jesus said: "What comes out of a man is what defiles a man. For from within, out of the heart of men, proceed evil thoughts, adultery, fornication, murder, theft, covetousness, wickedness, deceit, licentiousness, an evil eye, blasphemy, pride and foolishness. All these evil things come from within and defile a man" (Mark 7:20–23). And David wrote: "Who may ascend into the hill of the LORD? Or who may stand in His holy place? He who has clean hands and a pure heart, who has not lifted up his soul to an idol, nor sworn deceitfully. He shall receive blessing from the LORD, and righteousness from the God of his salvation" (Ps. 24:3–5, NKJV).

You can't stand in His holy place with hands contaminated with immorality and a heart polluted with sexual sin. But immorality is more than defiling—immorality is far more dangerous to your eternal soul. That's why Paul the Apostle cautioned the church at Corinth to flee from sexual immorality (1 Cor. 6:18) and told the church at Thessalonica that it is the will of God, for their sanctification, that they abstain from sexual immorality (1 Thess. 4:3–5).

The writer of Hebrews warned that God will judge the sexually immoral and adulterous (Heb. 13:4). What does that judgment look like? It has eternal implications if you don't repent. Paul admonishes, "For this you know, that no sexually immoral or impure person, or one who is greedy, who is an idolater, has any inheritance in the kingdom of Christ and of God" (Eph. 5:5). And again, "Do you not know that the unrighteous will not inherit the kingdom of God? Do not be deceived. Neither fornicators, nor idolaters, nor adulterers, nor homosexuals, nor sodomites, nor thieves, nor covetous, nor drunkards, nor revilers, nor extortioners will inherit the kingdom of God" (1 Cor. 6:9–10, NKJV).

Jezebel seeks to seduce you into sexual immorality by tapping into the lust of the flesh. Paul has the answer: "Therefore put to death the parts of your earthly nature: sexual immorality, uncleanness, inordinate affection, evil desire, and covetousness, which is idolatry. Because of these things, the wrath of God comes on the sons of disobedience. You also once walked in these, when you lived in them" (Col. 3:5–7).

The Bible has plenty more to say about immorality, and not just in warnings, but also through illustrations. Consider the devastation David faced when he committed sexual immorality with Bathsheba—his firstborn son died, and he had dysfunction in his family line ever after. Or what about Samson and Delilah? His fall into sexual immorality left him literally in bondage and blind. Can you see the spiritual parallels to that natural consequence? We also watched Solomon, the wisest man in the world, fall into sexual immorality. I submit to you that if Solomon, Samson, and David can fall, anyone can. Let's not think more highly of ourselves than we ought, but let us walk in the fear of the Lord.

The Blinding Impacts of Idolatry

Because seductive Jezebel understands that different people have different weaknesses, this spirit doesn't depend on immorality alone to woo your heart away from your beloved Jesus. No, this principality also relies on the idolatry in your heart. I won't go into all the high-profile church financial scandals rooted in greed, which the Bible equates to idolatry (Col. 3:5). You are probably familiar with many of them. But financial improprieties are almost as common, if not nearly as hurtful, as adulterous affairs.

Let's step back and define idolatry. The first and second commandments prohibit idolatry. The simplest definition of idolatry is the worship of idols. Of course, we're not forming golden calves or bowing down to wooden objects or praying to graven images in the twenty-first century church. We're more likely to form opinions of our pastors and set them up on pedestals, or bow a knee to mammon, or pray for our own will (rather than God's will) to be done. Idolatry is essentially putting anything before God or in the place of God, whether that's family, work, sports, entertainment—or some desire of your heart or hobby of your hands.

In today's age Psalm 135:15 is especially true: "The idols of the nations are silver and gold, the work of men's hands." Like Nimrod, who led the building of the tower of Babel, many people believe they don't need God. Some churches are even building massive followings without seeking God's will along the way. I believe idolatry is at the root of seeker-friendly churches where rock-star personalities are taking the rightful place of Jesus, and success and prosperity teachings are taking the place of the whole gospel, which requires much more from us than false gods.

But Isaiah prophesied of the foolishness of idolatry: "Those who make an image, all of them are useless, and their precious things shall not profit; they are their own witnesses; they neither see nor know, that they may be ashamed. Who would form a god or mold an image that profits him nothing?" (Isa. 44:9–10, NKJV). Idolatry gets you nowhere in the end. If you sow to the flesh—if you sow to your idolatry, which is a work of the flesh—you will reap corruption (Gal. 6.8). That's Bible.

John warned, "Little children, keep yourselves from idols" (1 John 5:21). Paul didn't warn the churches to flee only from sexual immorality; he also warned them to flee from idolatry (1 Cor. 10:14). Why? Because beyond reaping corruption, your sorrows will be multiplied if you chase after other gods (Ps. 16:4). Over and over again we read in Scripture that Israel's idol worship provoked the Lord to anger. Nevertheless, the Old Testament Jezebel worshipped idols—and the spirit that motivated the wicked woman to give false gods a place reserved solely for Jehovah God wants you to worship abominable idols too.

When we're trusting in our idols, we're not fully trusting in the Lord. That offends Him because He is trustworthy. The Lord is trustworthy in all He promises (Ps. 145:13). The decrees of the Lord are trustworthy (Ps. 19:7). The Word of the Lord is true, and everything He does is trustworthy (Ps. 33:4). That's why David hated those who regard useless idols and committed his trust to the Lord (Ps. 31:6). Jesus said you can't serve God and mammon (Matt. 6:24). You might just as well say that you can't serve God and your idol. The effect of idolatry is subtle, and it doesn't happen overnight, but what Jesus said is absolute truth: "No one can serve two masters. For either he will hate the one and love the other, or else he will hold to the one and despise the other. You cannot serve God and money" (Matt. 6:24).

Tearing Down Idols

Now is a good time to ask the Holy Spirit to show you any idols in your life. As you do, also ask the Lord to break off any deception in your mind. Deception has a blinding effect. You may be walking in deception and not even know it. Indeed, that is the nature of deception. If you knew you were deceived, you'd repent.

As you pray, consider what the psalmist revealed about idols and those who serve them: "They have mouths, but they cannot speak; eyes, but they cannot see; they have ears, but they cannot hear; noses, but they cannot smell; they have hands, but they cannot feel; feet, but they cannot walk; neither can they speak with their throat. Those who make them are like them; so is everyone who trusts in them" (Ps. 115:5–8).

If you are ready to rid yourself of idolatry, pray this prayer:

> *Father, I come to You in the name of Jesus. I ask You to reveal to me any idolatry in my heart. Show me, Lord, where I've allowed the enemy to seduce me into worshipping my own will, other gods, and even people. I ask You right now to make it clear to me, break the deception off my mind, and help me see. By Your grace, I will turn from it when You show me. I will repent and serve only You, in the name of Jesus. Amen.*

The Holy Spirit may not show you in this instant—or you may already see clearly some areas of idolatry that you need to rid from your heart even now. Either way, if and when you begin to realize you are serving idols move swiftly to do what the great kings and judges did in the Old Testament: tear them down.

Of course, this isn't an act of physically tearing down idols. In most cases, it's an act of tearing down the idols that you've erected in your heart. It will probably mean changing how you spend your time and money. As Ezekiel prophesied in Ezekiel 14:6, "Repent and turn away from your idols and turn away your faces from all your abominations." Remember what Jonah said when he received the revelation of his own rebellion while sitting in the belly of a great fish: "Those who regard worthless idols forsake their own Mercy" (Jon. 2:8, NKJV). Turn back to the Lord. He's waiting on you.

Now commit to restoring the first commandment to first place in your life. While Jezebel's agenda is to turn you away from your first love and seduce you into immorality and idolatry, the Holy Spirit's agenda is to establish the first commandment in first place in your life. Jesus said, "You shall love the Lord your God with all your heart, and with all your soul, and with all your mind.' This is the first and great commandment" (Matt. 22:36–38).

Don't Be the Victim in Jezebel's Master Plot

In the 1938 movie *Jezebel* that I mentioned at the beginning of this chapter, the character Bette Davis played was responsible for murder and mayhem. To be sure, Jezebel's master plot involves plenty of both. Jezebel is actively pursuing its victims. If you read Christian and secular news headlines with an understanding of how Jezebel truly operates, then you will see this spirit is finding plenty of success putting souls in bondage to immorality and idolatry. But there are many other victims that don't have the name recognition to make headlines. Everyday believers like you and me are just as much a target of Jezebel's seductions as rock-star preachers. Remember, Jesus said that Jezebel seduced His "servants." If you are saved, then you are a servant of God. That qualifies you as Jezebel's target.

Scripture is so clear. So how then is the spirit of Jezebel allowed to continue destroying lives, wreaking havoc in the church, and rising up in our media? For one thing—and it bears repeating—too many believers mistakenly relegate the Jezebel spirit's activities to "control" and "manipulation." Make no mistake, control and manipulation are merely surface-level traits of this wicked spirit. While much of the body of Christ wages all-out war against controlling people in the name of Jezebel, the real enemy works behind the scenes—unseen.

Let's face it: Jezebel is a demonic idol in the spiritual-warfare world. Many pastors and teachers without a true revelation of this spirit's deeper motives of seducing the saints to commit immorality and idolatry have picked up on the *Jezebel* buzzword in order to draw a crowd—or visitors to their websites. Indeed, incomplete teachings continue to circulate the Internet. Maybe you've seen some of the articles on how to recognize Jezebel, the ten traits of a Jezebel spirit, or even how to defeat Jezebel in twenty-four hours. There is good information in some of these articles, but flat-out error in most.

Meanwhile, the real Jezebel spirit is hiding behind the ignorant hype that guards the grander agenda of this ancient evil. Because we're ignorant of the devil's devices, we are not effectively waging war against the real Jezebel. We're just whacking at surface-level weeds this spirit throws out as a distraction. Some of the results: pastors keep falling into sexual immorality and idolatry even while people with strong personalities are falsely labeled Jezebels and ostracized.

Hear me: pastors and others will keeping falling into immorality and idolatry until the church understands the spirit that preys on these sins and refuses to tolerate it any longer. That means refusing to tolerate the lust in your own heart and refusing to tolerate immorality and idolatry in your church. You can't fight an enemy you can't see. That's what Jezebel is counting on. Take some time to understand your enemy. Pray for your pastor, and avoid the snares of Jezebel in your own life. You may not end up making headlines if you fall into sexual immorality or idolatry, but your compromise is just as devastating to God's heart.

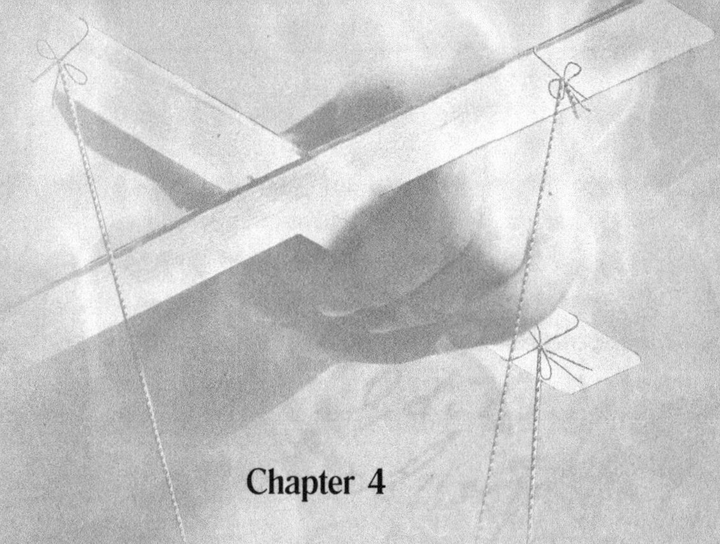

Chapter 4

AHAB THE EMPOWERER

PASTOR JIMMY WAS not in his best preaching form that Wednesday night. Making matters worse, the midweek service crowd was especially small, and latecomers straggling through the front door during worship were distracting people. Pastor Jimmy kept right on preaching his three-point message to a faithful few who were trying their best to track with him—but his message just wasn't hitting home, and at this rate the offering was likely to be small.

With desperation in his voice, Pastor Jimmy would call for the people to "Say amen!" and give him a "witness." But the faithful few were fidgeting in their seats, looking at their watches, and waiting for the man of God to finish his third closing. Suddenly Pastor Jimmy stopped dead in his tracks. This tough guy—a former wrestling champ—looked like he was going to break down and cry.

"You have offended the Holy Ghost, and you need to

repent!" he hollered at the congregation, choking back tears, before slamming his Bible shut and storming out of the sanctuary. Shocked, the congregation was silent for a moment until the associate pastor assumed the pulpit and continued rebuking the silent onlookers. The associate pastor heaped a few shovelfuls of guilt and condemnation on the faithful few before leading the confused congregation in a prayer of repentance.

The congregation went along with it, but the spiritual atmosphere was tense. Many people just wanted to leave but felt trapped by the intimidating display of church authority. No one there had ever seen anything like it—and no one knew what to do next. The associate pastor knew what to do: take up a guilt offering. Of course, it wasn't a guilt offering like we find in the Old Testament. (See Leviticus 5.) The associate pastor, though, surely tapped into the guilt that was attacking the minds of the people, for "grieving the Holy Spirit," to fill the church coffers.

Was Pastor Jimmy's mid-sermon tantrum really motivated by a grieved spirit that was jealous for God? Or was he just angry that his sermon wasn't getting a reaction that would motivate people to sow more money into the building fund? It was more the latter, and a few discerning saints caught on to the ploy. Nevertheless, this classic passive-aggressive behavior paid dividends for the temperamental Pastor Jimmy, whose outbursts were usually reserved for behind-the-scenes staff meetings. Pastor Jimmy was operating in a sulking, manipulative Ahab spirit that tag-teamed with a Jezebel spirit operating through the associate pastor to get him what he ultimately wanted—money.

In this chapter we'll take a closer look at Ahab, a political creature who married Jezebel to establish an alliance with her father. We'll also explore how Ahab empowers Jezebel to advance her master plot and what motivated him to engage in a poisonous one-act play that's been repeating itself for centuries. What you'll notice in the pages ahead is this: Ahab needed Jezebel to execute his will, and Jezebel needed Ahab for the purpose of power—but Jezebel ultimately pulled Ahab's strings, put words in his mouth, and carried out her agenda using his authority behind the scenes. As you read on, consider how these characters are examples of spirits that still operate in the earth today.

Ahab Unleashes Jezebel

The sulking scene I described at Pastor Jimmy's church reminded me of when Ahab pitched a hissy fit because Naboth wouldn't hand over his vineyard to the abominable king. Naboth the Jezreelite had a vineyard next to Ahab's palace—and Ahab wanted it. He asked Naboth politely and even put sugar on top: "Give me your vineyard, so that I can have it for a garden of herbs, because it is near to my house, and I will give you a better vineyard for it, or if you prefer, I will give you its worth in money" (1 Kings 21:2). Ahab fully anticipated Naboth would make a deal, but the Jezreelite refused him. Naboth wasn't just being hard to get along with. Naboth refused Ahab because the vineyard was part of his inheritance from his father.

In response to the flat-out rejection Ahab didn't scream and yell or make threats against Naboth. Ahab, rather, went home and pitched a fit in the king's chambers. The Bible says he "went into his house sullen and displeased" (v. 4, NKJV). Ahab climbed into bed and refused to eat a morsel. He lay there depressed and sullen because Naboth rejected him—refusing to give in to the king's entitlement attitude and taking a firm stand for what rightfully belonged to him.

Why was Ahab so distraught over a patch of land when he had most of the kingdom at his disposal? Beyond idolizing his own desires, Ahab's depressive state was a passive response designed to win the attention of an aggressive ally who could get him what he wanted. That aggressor, of course, was his wicked wife, Jezebel. When weak-and-pitiful Ahab sulked and complained to power-hungry Jezebel, she saw a golden opportunity to usurp his authority and let the inner circle know who was really running the show. Queen Jezebel assured Ahab she would deliver the land and encouraged him to let his heart be cheerful (v. 7).

Jezebel Puts Words in Ahab's Mouth

Of course, Ahab had no idea what Jezebel had up her sleeve, and Naboth never saw Jezebel's attack coming. Naboth had no reason to believe Ahab was going to retaliate by unleashing the murderous Jezebel against him over a patch of land. Naboth didn't know that the woman who killed the prophets had him in her crosshairs. Let's unpack these next verses so we can see how Ahab and Jezebel worked together:

> So she wrote letters in Ahab's name and sealed them with his seal and sent the letters to the elders and to the nobles that were in the city where Naboth lived.
>
> —1 KINGS 21:8

Notice in this verse how Jezebel usurped Ahab's authority. Ahab didn't tell her how to—or how not to—go about getting Naboth's field. When he empowered Jezebel to go after what he wanted, he lost all control over the tactics she would use to deliver on her promise. But think about it for a minute. If Ahab had wanted Naboth killed and his vineyard added to the royal estate, he could have ordered a soldier in his army to handle the task for him.

Murder wasn't likely on his mind, yet he must have known Jezebel might resort to murder to get the job done. After all, she had the prophets of Jehovah executed to spread her idolatrous religion in the land without godly protest. Ahab was passive—even with Jezebel. He did nothing to stop her when she had the prophets massacred, and he would do nothing to stop her from murdering Naboth. He just let her do as she pleased, as long as it suited his purposes.

Scripture shows that Ahab was more than capable of talking, but Jezebel sometimes put words in his mouth. Ahab didn't mind because at times he was insecure about speaking for himself; he was too fearful of rejection to risk making waves. In the Naboth incident Jezebel wrote words in Ahab's name with no evidence that Ahab even knew what she was doing. The contents of Jezebel's letter read:

> Proclaim a fast, and set Naboth on high among the people, and set two men, sons of Belial, before him, to bear witness against him, saying, "You blasphemed God and the king." And then carry him out and stone him, so that he will die.
>
> —1 KINGS 21:9–10

These scriptures are rich with revelation on how the Jezebel spirit operates. Consider Jezebel's modus operandi. Jezebel flatters to get what she wants. Remember, the Jezebel spirit is essentially a seducing spirit, and flattery is a tool in the hands of the seducer. In Ahab's name Jezebel flattered Naboth "with high honor among the people" (v. 12, NKJV). Naboth goes down in Bible history as one who fell victim to Jezebel's seduction through flattery—and it cost him his life. The flattery ultimately gave way to false accusations that got him killed. It was a setup in the spirit.

Remember, Jezebel needed Ahab to execute her plan. Well, at least she needed his name. In a church setting this looks like a department head or associate pastor who wants everyone to know how much favor they have with the senior pastor. The implication is that they are in an inner circle and you would do well to go along with their plans so you can find favor with the senior pastor too. If that doesn't work, Jezebel tries to intimidate you by suggesting she's sure the pastor (or boss at work, head of the family, and so on) will be upset if you don't step in line with what's she's proposing.

We'll talk more about that in a minute. Right now let's watch and see how Jezebel executed her murderous plan:

"The men of his city, the elders and the nobles who lived in his city, did as Jezebel had sent word to them, as it was written in the letters that she had sent to them" (v. 11).

Jezebel Deceives Naboth's Best Friends

Jezebel usually works in cooperation with others. Here she strong-armed city leaders, as well as the elders and nobles who were inhabitants of the city, in Ahab's name. It wasn't hard for Jezebel to trick the people of the city by announcing a feast in Naboth's honor. Apparently Naboth was a pretty good guy, and they deemed him worthy of honor.

The men of his city, along with the elders and the nobles, went right along with Jezebel's plan. This happens a lot in churches, workplaces, and even in homes. Unless you understand how Jezebel operates, you are likely to fall victim to these types of ploys. The Bible says they proclaimed a fast and that Naboth was seated in a place of honor among his fellow kinsmen (v. 12). That's when it happened—and neither Naboth nor his kinsmen saw it coming:

> Two men, children of Belial, came in and sat in front of him, and the men of Belial witnessed against Naboth in the presence of the people, saying, "Naboth blasphemed God and the king." Then they carried him out of the city and stoned him to death. Then they sent word to Jezebel, saying, "Naboth has been stoned and is dead."
>
> —1 Kings 21:13–14

The King James Version of this verse calls the scoundrels "men of Belial." *Belial* comes from the Hebrew word *beliyyaal*, which means "worthless, good-for-nothing, unprofitable, base fellow, wicked, ruin and destruction."[1] The men of Belial are among Jezebel's puppets. These are Jezebel's hired hatchet men. She likely paid them a fair sum to throw Naboth under the bus.

It has always amazed me how quickly Naboth's kinsmen turned on him. Didn't the irony in his being honored one minute and accused the next occur to them? From this we see that the Jezebel spirit has its way of turning even your close friends against you. Jezebel murders the reputations of those who get in its way. I've experienced this firsthand.

I was once involved in a church that focused heavily on dominionism and spiritual warfare. Spiritual abuse at the hands of Jezebel and Ahab ran rampant, but most people didn't see it because, ironically, the leadership preached fervently against these and other spirits. More than once I was honored among the congregation at banquets—including being given special seating as Naboth had received. Kind words were offered about my dedication to God.

Ironically the beginning of the end of my time at that church came at a special event at which one of the senior leaders put me in the hot seat in front of several dozen elders and falsely accused me of neglecting my responsibilities in the wake of a legitimate family emergency about which he was well aware. I had been stoned in the spirit and limped out not knowing what hit me until months later. I did, however, know it was coming. The Holy Spirit told me what was about to happen—that I was going to be lambasted in front of the group. I wanted to skip the event and go home, but He told me to walk through it.

It was unpleasant, but I'm convinced the Holy Spirit had me endure it so that I could see how Jezebel and Ahab work in tandem to murder those who don't give them what they want. From that day forward some in the church felt sorry for me. Others kept their distance, seeing as I had suddenly turned from celebrated leader to *persona non grata* virtually overnight. The pastor, meanwhile, never looked me in the eye again. I stayed in that church, trying for months to find a way to get back in his good graces, but he only gave me the cold shoulder. Talk about passive-aggressive behavior!

When Ahab Lets Jezebel Set You Up

Has Jezebel ever set you up in the spirit? Ahab could have been behind it. We just saw how this dynamic passive-aggressive duo can cause even your best friends to turn on you—the men of Naboth's city, as well as the elders and the nobles, went right along with Jezebel's plan. There's no evidence that anyone even protested Naboth's stoning, much less came to his defense, when Jezebel's scoundrels falsely accused him. This was the same guy they were celebrating just moments before the men of Belial executed Jezebel's plan.

When I left the abusive church—a church that preached against Jezebel with a passion—I was spiritually crucified. I lost every friend I had in that church (until some of them later realized what was going on and came to me privately to repent and rekindle the relationship). A close friend launched false accusations against me, calling me an uncaring, unloving, unfit mother for leaving the church because my daughter was rooted there. Other close friends accused me of having a python spirit. One of my spiritual mentors said there was a Jezebel spirit transposed over my body. I was labeled with spirits of rebellion, pride, and more.

I hung up the phone after talking to one "friend" and wondered how it was possible for one person to be (supposedly) filled with so many demons yet allowed to get up Sunday morning and teach in the church. I mean, how was one who was celebrated and honored and given authority over souls one week labeled a spiritual monster the next week by people with whom she had labored intensely for years without issue? Was this really a horrible lack of discernment on the part of leadership who had, for nearly a decade, made it clear to the congregation that I was one of the most accurate prophetic voices they had heard? Or was there something else working behind the scenes?

Looking back, I see now that Jezebel attacked because I would no longer cooperate with its agenda. I was no longer willing to feed my gifts, talents, and money to the demons—the Jezebels, Ahabs, eunuchs, and children of Belial that had infiltrated the church system—at the expense of neglecting my family. When I began to point out problems in the way people were being treated, I became the problem and was sorely mistreated myself. Jezebel had turned on me. Jezebel will turn on you too if you don't give it what it wants. Once you are no longer an asset to Jezebel's puppet show, it writes your death scene.

This does not always manifest in the natural; sometimes it's just spiritual warfare. But other times that spiritual warfare enters the natural realm. Remember when Jezebel threatened Elijah? Elijah had just killed all her false prophets. When Jezebel found out, she sent a messenger to Elijah saying, "So let the gods do to me and more also, if I do not make your life as the life of one of them by tomorrow about this time" (1 Kings 19:2). Well, Jezebel didn't win that round but the spirit of Jezebel targeted the spirit of Elijah during Jesus's days on the earth—and used Ahab to do it. Consider the scene:

> But when Herod's birthday was celebrated, the daughter of Herodias danced before them and pleased Herod. Therefore he promised with an oath to give her whatever she would ask. Being previously instructed by her mother, she said, "Give me John the Baptist's head on a platter."
>
> The king was sorry. Nevertheless, for the oath's sake and those who sat with him at supper, he commanded it to be given to her. He sent and beheaded John in the prison. His head was brought on a platter and given to the girl, and she brought it to her mother. His disciples came and took up the body and buried it. And they went and told Jesus.
>
> —Matthew 14:6–12

Herod was a passive character under the influence of an Ahab spirit, and Herodias was an aggressive character under the influence of a Jezebel spirit. In Matthew 17:10–13 Jesus said John the Baptist was carrying the spirit of Elijah. Jezebel got its revenge on Elijah in this scene—and used the Ahab spirit to do it. That is, the spirit of Jezebel cut off the voice of John the Baptist—the one moving in a spirit of Elijah to turn the hearts of the fathers to their children and the hearts of the children to their fathers (Mal. 4:6). And the spirit of Jezebel used the spirit of Ahab's influence over Herod to execute the murderous plot.

Jezebel Gets No Blood on Her Hands

Jezebel rarely gets blood on her hands. She doesn't have to. She manipulates her cast of hatchet-carrying puppets to do the bloody work. After aggressive Jezebel used others to effectively steal Naboth's land for passive Ahab, she was thrilled to deliver news of the conquest. The Bible says Jezebel heard that Naboth had been stoned and was dead. It's probable that Jezebel heard this from one of her eunuchs. We'll talk more about Jezebel's eunuchs and the role they play in her dark kingdom in an upcoming chapter. Let's read the end of Naboth's account:

> When Jezebel heard that Naboth had been stoned and was dead, she said to Ahab, "Arise, take possession of the vineyard of Naboth the Jezreelite, which he refused to sell to you for money, for Naboth is not alive, but dead." When Ahab heard that Naboth was dead, he got up to go down to the vineyard of Naboth the Jezreelite, to take possession of it.
>
> —1 Kings 21:15–16

Oh, what satisfaction Jezebel must have felt in that moment! She once again proved her worth to Ahab, which would give her even more influence in his kingdom. Ahab just received a gift horse, and he wasn't about to look it in the mouth. In other words, he wasn't going to ask her how she got the field; all that mattered was that it was now his. He was grateful for it. He was no longer depressed, no longer complaining. He was ready to go possess the land—and Jezebel was happy to let him have this joy. See, there are rewards to serving Jezebel from a natural perspective. Jezebel doesn't expect you to serve her agenda without your due reward. But it's all a façade. The end of any cooperation with Jezebel is destruction. We'll talk about that more in a later chapter.

For now notice that Jezebel herself did not go down and take possession of the land. She didn't really have any interest in the land. Her interest was in maintaining control over her husband. By giving him the honor of taking the land, she fed his low self-esteem and kept him coming back for more. Jezebel is willing to share the glory with Ahab, but only if it serves her purposes. In this situation it served her well, and her hands remained clean despite her murderous orchestration because Ahab tolerated her.

Maybe you've seen these types of situations play out in your life. This can manifest on the job with a coworker the boss uses to fire underperforming employees or handle sticky personnel issues that demand reprimands. The boss is flowing in an Ahab spirit. He doesn't want to look like the bad guy. He doesn't want to confront the issue. So he uses a Jezebelic coworker to handle those tasks for him. The problem is the Jezebelic coworker feeds the Ahab boss information that's far from accurate about people she doesn't like. The Jezebelic coworker manipulates Ahab into giving her the authority to fire people for what are actually false offenses. Jezebel doesn't get blood on her hands because she reprimands and fires people in the boss's name.

This happens in churches and families, too. It displeases the Lord. The Lord ultimately holds Ahab responsible. Immediately after Ahab took possession of the land, the word of the Lord came to Elijah: "Arise, go down to meet Ahab, king of Israel, who is in Samaria. He is now in the vineyard of Naboth, where he has gone down to possess it. You shall speak to him, saying, 'Thus says the LORD: Have you killed and also taken possession?' And you shall speak to him, saying, 'Thus says the LORD: In the place where dogs licked the blood of Naboth, dogs will lick your own blood!'" (1 Kings 21:18–19).

Notice how the Lord pins the murder on Ahab. Jezebel's name is nowhere mentioned. This is one of the dangers of handing over your authority to Jezebel. The Lord gave you the authority you walk in—all authority comes from God (Rom. 13:1), and Christ specifically gave you His authority (Matt. 10:1; Luke 10:19). If you hand that authority over to Jezebel or any other spirit, the blame still lies on you. You are responsible for what you do with your delegated authority. You can't blame Jezebel for tricking you or intimidating you or seducing you. God won't hear it. He will, of course, forgive you if you repent. He even gave Jezebel a space to repent, but she would not (Rev. 2:21).

God had put up with plenty from Ahab, who goes down in biblical history as the king who did more to provoke the Lord than any other. But handing over his authority to Jezebel to have an innocent man murdered was seemingly the straw that broke the camel's back. God judged Ahab—He would later judge Jezebel.

Tolerating That Woman Jezebel

Ahab tolerates sin—idolatry, sexual immorality, murder, and anything else Jezebel does in the camp. Consider what Jesus said to the church at Thyatira:

> I have a few things against you: You permit that woman Jezebel, who calls herself a prophetess, to teach and seduce My servants to commit sexual immorality and eat food sacrificed to idols. I gave her time to repent of her sexual immorality, but she did not repent. Look! I will throw her onto a sickbed, and those who commit adultery with her into great tribulation, unless they repent of their deeds. I will put her children to death, and all the churches shall know that I am He who searches the hearts and minds. I will give to each one of you according to your deeds.
>
> —Revelation 2:20–23

Jesus made it very clear that He would cast Jezebel into a sickbed—and her puppets too—unless they repented. In the Book of Revelation Jesus is talking about people who cooperate with the spirit of Jezebel, but the Lord executed this same judgment on Queen Jezebel and Ahab. The eunuchs escaped because they threw Jezebel down. Ahab died in battle, and it was just as Elijah had prophesied:

> A certain man drew a bow at random and struck the king of Israel between the joints of the armor, and because of this, he said to the driver of his chariot, "Turn around and carry me out of the battle, for I am wounded." The battle intensified that day, and the king was propped up in his chariot against the Arameans and died that evening, and the blood ran out of the wound into the floor of the chariot. A proclamation went throughout the army as the sun was setting, saying, "Every man is to return to his city, and every man is to return to his own country."
>
> So the king died and was brought to Samaria, and they buried him there. The chariot was washed in the pool of Samaria, and the dogs licked up the king's blood, and they washed his armor according to the word which the LORD spoke.
>
> —1 KINGS 22:34–38

What about Jezebel and her children? We'll look more closely at this account in a later chapter, but for now suffice it to say that Jehu confronted her, the eunuchs betrayed her, and she died. Jehu, who would later become king, went on to wipe out the children of Jezebel and Ahab, but the passive-aggressive couple's legacy lives on, and the spirits that influenced them are still operating in the church and the world today.

Again, Ahab did more to provoke the Lord to anger than any other king before him. He married Jezebel and started worshipping other gods. Ahab's idol worship led him into great deception. He may have sat on the throne and worn the royal signet ring, but Jezebel ruled and reigned the kingdom of Israel much of the time. Ahab did more than tolerate Jezebel, which would have been bad enough. Ahab empowered Jezebel. It's important to remember this: as evil as Ahab was in the eyes of the Lord, ultimately he was a willing victim of Jezebel in a deadly codependent relationship.

Passive-Aggressive Codependents in Action

Although Jezebel is the aggressor of this corrupt codependent couple, Ahab is aggressive in his own right—just not outwardly so. Understanding the concept of codependency is vital to recognizing the Jezebel-Ahab dynamic. *Merriam-Webster's* defines *codependency* as a "psychological condition or a relationship in which a person is controlled or manipulated by another who is affected with a pathological condition"; or, more broadly, "dependence on the needs of or control by another."[2]

Ahab was dependent on Jezebel's control, and Jezebel was dependent on Ahab's needs. Together they ebbed and flowed to get what they wanted from each other—and to get each other to do what they wanted. Codependency isn't reserved for Jezebel-Ahab type relationships. You can be codependent without coming under the influence of a Jezebel or an Ahab spirit. But where you find Jezebel, you often find a codependent Ahab and vice versa.

In the 1 Kings 21 account we witnessed passive-aggressive codependents in action. Jezebel executed her aggressive plan perfectly, using passive Ahab, fearful eunuchs, and others to do away with her opposition. Although these individuals were clearly influenced by spirits, modern psychology attempts to explain these behaviors, and we can learn plenty about the workings of Jezebel and Ahab from a quick study.

According to research from Mental Health America (MHA), a person with a passive-aggressive behavior pattern "may appear to comply or act appropriately, but actually behaves negatively and passively resists."[3] This is what Ahab did when Naboth told him no. On the surface he seemed to comply with Naboth's wishes and went away peacefully. But he behaved negatively—climbing into bed and refusing to eat—in passive resistance.

There are several symptoms of passive-aggressive personality disorder. These include a contradictory and inconstant behavior: "A person with this behavior pattern may appear enthusiastic to carry out others' requests, but purposely performs in a manner that is not useful and sometimes even damaging."[4] This characterizes Ahab's entire reign. He accepted the crown and committed to keeping a covenant with the Lord, only to marry a foreign woman who brought foreign gods into the land. He then went on to give her authority that didn't belong to her, and she used it to kill the prophets of Jehovah and innocent Naboth.

Passive-aggressive personality disorder is also characterized by intentional avoidance of responsibility: "Some behaviors that may be used to avoid responsibility include: procrastination—to delay or postpone needlessly and intentionally; deliberate inefficiency—purposefully performing in an incompetent manner; forgetfulness."[5] Finally, MHA lists several other traits, many of which you can apply directly to Ahab just from the Naboth incident alone.

For example, MHA points to "feelings of resentment

bitterness

toward others."[6] Ahab resented Naboth for not handing over his vineyard. Stubbornness is another passive-aggressive trait. Ahab was stubborn against God's will. Passive-aggressive people also tend to be argumentative. Ahab argued with Elijah, calling him his "enemy" (1 Kings 21:20) and a troubler of Israel (1 Kings 18:17). They have unexpressed anger or hostility. Ahab never expressed his anger or hostility toward Naboth—he let Jezebel handle it. MHA's list of characteristics of passive-aggressives include being easily offended, being resentful of useful suggestions from others, blaming others, being sulky, and being chronically impatient.[7]

Again, keep in mind, please, that not everyone who manifests passive-aggressive traits has an Ahab or Jezebel spirit. You may just be dealing with an immature person who saw that type of behavior modeled on the home front or in the workplace and adopted the pattern unknowingly. But where you find Jezebel and Ahab, you will find these traits manifesting. Passive-aggressive traits—arguing, resenting, blaming, sulking, impatience—are essentially works of the flesh but can be fortified by demon spirits if we do not work with the Holy Spirit to grow in the grace of Christ. When we embrace rather than reject the flaws in our souls, the Holy Spirit shows us we are walking on dangerous ground.

In the next chapter we'll look more closely at some of the ways we may be empowering Jezebel in our own lives and how to unravel this soul tie.

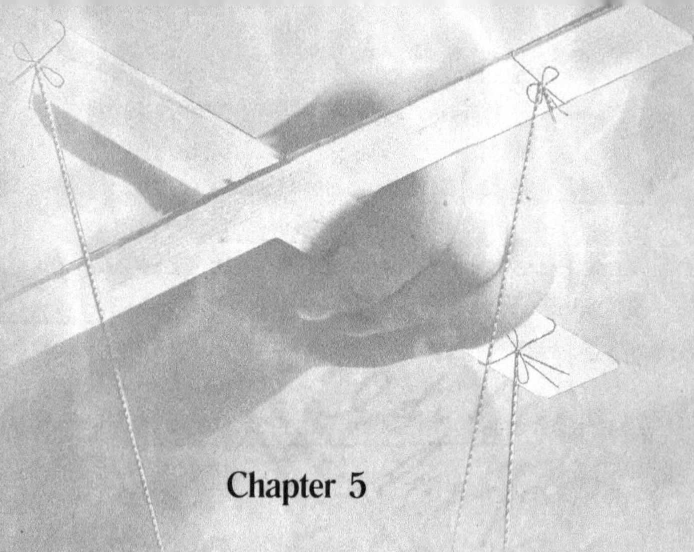

Chapter 5

UNRAVELING AHAB'S ALLIANCES

When you think of politicians, a long list of stereotypes probably comes to mind. The stereotypical politician is a power-hungry, dishonest, manipulative promise-breaker who seeks his own agenda at the expense of those he serves. The stereotypical politician is selfish, corrupt, hypocritical, and easily swayed by large financial contributions. The stereotypical politician is more concerned with what you can do for him than what he can do for you.

Although all politicians don't fit that bill, King Ahab would move well in many modern-day political circles. King Ahab was clearly power hungry, dishonest, and manipulative. He was a covenant-breaker who sought his own agenda at the expense of those he was called to serve. He was selfish, corrupt, double-minded, and easily swayed by the opinions of others. Indeed, King Ahab was more concerned with what people could do for him than what he could do for people.

Those troubling traits remind me of Paul's prophesy about perilous times in the last days: "Men will be lovers of themselves, lovers of money, boastful, proud, blasphemers, disobedient to parents, unthankful, unholy, without natural affection, truce breakers, slanderers, unrestrained, fierce, despisers of those who are good, traitors, reckless, conceited, lovers of pleasures more than lovers of God, having a form of godliness, but denying its power. Turn away from such people" (2 Tim. 3:2–5).

Ahab and Jezebel had a form of godliness—they worshipped gods—but they were anything but godly. These wicked monarchs were the kids of politicians. Notably, Jezebel was the daughter of a false prophet—King Ethbaal, the priest of Baal—and Astarte. (*Ethbaal* literally means "toward the idol" or "with Baal."[1]) Ahab was not ignorant of his sin in marrying Jezebel or in allowing her to set up idols to Baal in Israel—or in serving and worshipping these false gods (1 Kings 16:31). Ahab committed these abominations to please Jezebel. Ahab knew better, but his pursuit of political power caused him to break his promise to the One who set him in the seat of power: Jehovah.

Ahab sought political alliances to strengthen his command, but he had no true loyalty to those he aligned with. Beyond Ahab's marriage to Jezebel to reinforce diplomatic ties with Ethbaal, the king of Tyre, he also forged an opportunistic alliance with King Jehoshaphat to take land from Aram. Full of compromise, Ahab was willing to allow Jezebel to bring false gods into Israel and willing to sacrifice Jehoshaphat's life for his own as long as it served his selfish purposes. In other words, although Ahab needed alliances to forward his wicked agenda, Ahab had no loyalty to anyone but himself. The spirit we call Ahab operates in the same way.

In the last chapter we learned what motivates Ahab: power. We saw how Ahab used Jezebel to do his dirty work and how Ahab lets Jezebel set you up for a fall in a deadly passive-aggressive dynamic. In this chapter we'll use these revelations as a backdrop to discern how the Ahab spirit moves in your midst, how to recognize Ahab-like tendencies in your own soul, how to uproot the Ahab-Jezebel alliance, and ultimately how to combat Ahab attacks against your life.

How Ahab Moves in Your Midst

We've discussed how Ahab empowers Jezebel to kill, steal, and destroy. Jezebel had authority in the kingdom of Israel unrivaled by any queen before or after her. We also know Ahab funds Jezebel's idolatry and immorality. The royal palace had 850 false prophets on its payroll who ate at Jezebel's table (1 Kings 18:19) while true prophets were eating bread and drinking water in musky caves. But beyond empowering and funding Jezebel, there are many practical ways to recognize Ahab moving in your midst.

Now, let me preface this section with a friendly warning: there are far too many checklists on the Internet claiming a long list of Ahab-like traits without any scriptural reference. I'm cautious about such lists because, although I do believe experience—and even the Holy Spirit—can reveal strategies of the enemy that aren't necessarily recorded in Scripture, these lists often arm witch hunters to tag people with labels they don't deserve.

Those labels can be hurtful and actually open people up to attack by the very spirits that are erroneously pinned on them. In other words, calling someone a Jezebel can open the door for a wound that lets Jezebel in. Therefore, for the sake of our study, I prefer to keep any list of earmarks in line with the Word of God. Also keep in mind that just because someone has one or more of these traits does not automatically mean that person is operating in an Ahab spirit. You ultimately need Holy Spirit discernment.

Ahab is passive.

Ahab didn't hand over the kingdom to Jezebel officially, but he essentially stood by passively as she ran roughshod over God's plan for the nation. We see this same spirit of passivity in Adam, when he followed Eve into sin rather than exercising his authority in the garden. We also see passivity at work in the priest Eli, who would not put his foot down with his sinful sons. Lot was also passive, pitching his tent toward Sodom and eventually sitting in the midst of sin day in and day out. Ahab is a passive spirit that uses Jezebel as its aggressive counterpart.

Ahab is a power-hungry abuser.

Ahab is a political creature that's highly motivated by power. We see this in his decision to marry an idolatrous priest's daughter for political gain. We also witness his abuse of power as true prophets of God and Naboth are murdered, among other injustices.

In his classic book *Moby Dick* Herman Melville picked traits from King Ahab to personify Captain Ahab in his pursuit of a white whale. In *C. L. R. James: A Political Biography*, author Kent Worcester notes: "Ahab in particular is singled out as signifying the essentially totalitarian impulse concealed behind capitalism's relentless pursuit of conquest and expansion. In his mad hunt for the white whale, Ahab loses his humanity. A power-hungry renegade from civilization, he lords over his subordinates just as he seeks to dominate technology and nature."[2]

I've been in spiritually abusive churches where the quest for power turned living souls into rungs on a ladder to be stepped on and climbed over. Although many talk about Jezebel's eunuchs, let's remember that royal eunuchs—who could be likened to victims of abuse—served in Ahab's kingdom. To drive his political agenda, Ahab also submitted Israel to idol worship, thereby setting them up for eternal judgment.

Ahab is dishonest.

Like some politicians, Ahab is dishonest and uses dishonesty for his gain. Ahab allowed Jezebel to lie about Naboth, have him stoned, and steal his vineyard. Ahab allowed Jezebel to cut off the voice of the true prophets in the land. Ahab even had Micaiah jailed for telling the truth (1 Kings 22:24–28). Ahab was not a lover of the truth (2 Thess. 2:10) and saw lovers of the truth like Micaiah and Elijah as troublemakers and enemies (1 Kings 18:17, 21:20). I find it almost humorous that God would send a lying spirit into the mouth of Ahab's false prophets to usher in his disaster (1 Kings 22:22–23).

Maybe you've run into people with a lying spirit in their mouths or those who use dishonest means for their own gain. You know who I am talking about—the one at work who takes credit for the accomplishments of others and beefs up his reports to make his results look better than they really are. Or the one who deceitfully calls in sick so he can avoid a pressure-cooker meeting, leaving his coworkers to take the heat from the boss. You could be dealing with a power-hungry, covetous Ahab spirit.

When I consider the ways of Ahab in the Naboth incident, I'm reminded of Jeremiah 9:8: "Their tongue is an arrow shot out; it speaks deceit; one speaks peaceably to his neighbor with his mouth, but in his heart he lies in wait" (NKJV). If you're dealing with a dishonest Ahab, put it in God's hands—and pray for the person's deliverance. Remember, "The integrity of the upright will guide them, but the perverseness of transgressors will destroy them" (Prov. 11:3).

Ahab is a covetous coward.

We know that Ahab was covetous, desiring Naboth's land to the point of murder (1 Kings 21). But mixed in with that covetousness is cowardice. Ahab didn't have the gumption to carry out a plot against Naboth himself. He empowered Jezebel to do it. But that's not the only example we see in Scripture of Ahab's cowardice.

When Ahab made an alliance with Judah's King Jehoshaphat, the prophet Micaiah essentially prophesied that he would die in battle (see 1 Kings 22:17). Before the two kings went up to Ramoth Gilead to take the land from Aram, Ahab said, "'I will disguise myself and enter into the battle, but you wear your robes.' And the king of Israel disguised himself and went into the battle" (1 Kings 22:30). Ahab probably reasoned that he would be safe in his disguise and the enemy would go after King Jehoshaphat. He was right, as the next verse reveals the Aram king ordered his thirty-two chariot commanders not to fight with anyone except the king of Israel—and almost mistook Jehoshaphat for Ahab.

Although Ahab was in an alliance with Jehoshaphat, he was willing to watch him die on the battlefield to preserve his own wicked kingship. God is not a man that He should lie, though, and Micaiah was not a false prophet who told Ahab what he wanted to hear. Ahab was wounded in battle and died, just like Micaiah prophesied (vv. 34–37). Dogs licked up his blood, just as Elijah said they would (1 Kings 21:17–19).

The Ahab spirit is a cowering spirit. It will not take a forthright stand for what it believes but will use dishonesty, manipulation, and political alliances to get what it wants. You may have run into someone influenced by the Ahab spirit. This person often avoids coming out and saying what they want for fear of being rejected. Instead, they may manipulate other people to deliver what they long for on a silver platter, as Ahab did with his depressive state in Jezebel's presence after Naboth rejected his request for the vineyard.

Ahab is manipulative.

Jezebel is typically pegged as a spirit of control and manipulation, but Ahab is certainly a master of manipulation in his own right. Ahab even knows how to manipulate Jezebel to do his will. So while Ahab is Jezebel's puppet, Ahab also knows how to pull Jezebel's strings. Ahab's manipulation was based in his cowardice. For example, he manipulated Jehoshaphat into wearing king's robes in combat while he wore a plain army uniform because he was not brave enough to face the battle in light of Micaiah's prophecy. But Ahab could not ultimately manipulate God's Word and died in the end. Manipulation is not always a spiritual force. Many times it's just the flesh wanting what it wants and being willing to compromise God's Word to get it.

Ahab is a compromiser who tolerates sin.

Ahab tolerated Jezebel. He compromised the Word of God for his own political gain by sanctioning and even funding idolatry and immorality through the worship of false gods. This is a major problem in churches today. Pastors generally believe same-sex marriage and abortion are wrong, for example, but most of them won't talk to their congregations about it for fear of losing members.

According to researcher George Barna, less than 10 percent of pastors will speak to key issues of the day even though they agree the Bible speaks to every one of them. Most pastors are passive, willing to do "almost nothing" to get people active in politics. "Controversy keeps people from being in the seats, controversy keeps people from giving money, from attending programs,"

George Barna said on America Family Radio's *Today's Issues* broadcast.[3]

Ahab is an idolatrous covenant breaker.

Ahab served Baal (1 Kings 16:31), which makes him a rebellious covenant breaker because God clearly said, "You shall have no other gods before Me" (Exod. 20:3). By doing so, he set an example for all of Israel. This applies to our churches and our homes. When spiritual leaders or family leaders put anything before God, they are leading people into idolatry. Jezebel is often painted with the idolatrous brush, but the fact is that Jezebel led Ahab into idolatry and then Ahab led the people of Israel into idolatry by sanctioning idol worship in Israel.

Idolatry is not confined to Jezebel and Ahab spirits. Idolatry is a key strategy of the enemy. It has infiltrated our society at many levels—and it's deadly. Keep in mind: "Those who chase after other gods, their sorrows will be multiplied; their drink offerings of blood I will not offer, nor lift their names on my lips" (Ps. 16:4). Ask the Holy Spirit to show you if there is any idolatry in your life and turn away from it and back to the living God.

Ahab is a corrupt corruptor.

Ahab was corrupt on many levels. He was spiritually corrupt, serving idols. He was morally corrupt, allowing Jezebel to murder the prophets and Naboth. He was politically corrupt, using Jehoshaphat for his own political gain and forming an alliance with Jezebel's idolatrous father. But Ahab was not only corrupt, he was also a corruptor. He helped Jezebel bring corruption into Israel.

Someone under the influence of an Ahab spirit is not

content for you to condone or facilitate their sin. They want you to join in with them. You see this in any form of peer pressure. Although Ahab demanded Micaiah to tell him the truth, Ahab's false prophets pressured Micaiah to prophesy falsely: "See here, the words of the prophets unanimously declare success for the king. Please let your word be like the word of one of them, and speak that which is good" (1 Kings 22:13). Ahab surrounds himself with corrupt corruptors.

Ahab is double-minded.

Ahab is easily swayed by the opinions of others because he's a people pleaser at heart who fears rejection. It didn't take any time at all for Ahab to let Jezebel convince him to set up Baal and Ashtoreth worship in Israel. Ahab worshipped Jehovah and the false gods too. He was double-minded. But Jesus said, "No one can serve two masters. For either he will hate the one and love the other, or else he will hold to the one and despise the other" (Matt. 6:24), and James 1:8 assures us that "a double-minded man is unstable in all his ways."

Ahab is emotionally unstable.

Ahab was an emotional train wreck. He wore his heart on his sleeve when he wasn't getting what he wanted, like an immature teenager. Ahab got angry and depressed when Naboth refused to sell his inheritance (1 Kings 21:4). He was insecure about the will of the Lord and kept false prophets around him to assure him he was on the right track (1 Kings 22). He was led by his emotions and his flesh—and false prophets—instead of being led by the Spirit of God.

How Ahab Spirits Get In

We could go on and on with characteristics of Ahab, and you'll notice there's plenty of overlap among the traits of this wicked king from which we draw the name of this passive-aggressive spirit. But how does the spirit of Ahab find entrance into our souls? And how do we recognize if we're operating in an Ahab spirit?

The answer to the second question is found in the list above. If you are double-minded, emotionally unstable, have a tendency to be passive-aggressive rather than assertive, manipulate and tolerate sin, you need to cooperate with the Holy Spirit to root these things out of your life. It could be Ahab or it could be Jezebel or it could be some other spirit influencing your behavior—or it could be your flesh leaning on learned behavior. Ultimately I'm not as concerned with what it's called as I am with rooting it out. Sometimes it seems easier to deal with a spirit we can name, but ultimately sin is sin, and we need to root it out of our hearts in a hurry.

Now let's answer the first question. How does Ahab get in? I believe Ahab gets in much like any other opportunistic spirit gets in: through hurts and wounds, through rejection, through fear, through generational curses, or through learned behavior. If you grew up in a home where Ahab and Jezebel ruled, for example, then you are likely to pick up on behavior patterns that displease God. You may not be officially operating in an Ahab or Jezebel spirit, but you may be mimicking the behavior, and if you don't repent, these spirits can come in to reinforce your fleshly habits.

Remember, Ahab had a passive spirit and used Jezebel's aggression to compensate for his passivity. In his book *Discerning and Defeating the Ahab Spirit* Steve Sampson says, "Those of us with Ahab-like tendencies need to repent of our passive behaviors and ask the Holy Spirit to reveal the root of this lifestyle and show us how we became trapped in it. Passivity is a spiritual problem. It stems from the fear of man—a self-abasement scenario of not caring enough to embrace our own dignity as redeemed human beings. This comes not from the perfect identity of our human spirit, which is whole and complete in Christ, but from our imperfect soul, which needs to be restored."[4]

Are You Codependent on Jezebel?

Codependent personalities, which often plague people with low self-esteem, are also open doors for Jezebel and Ahab—and other spirits. Not all codependent relations are Jezebel-Ahab relationships, but those spirits can easily become an influence. Mental Health America (MHA) lists seventeen characteristics of codependent people. Read over this list and ask the Holy Spirit to show you if you are in a codependent relationship:

1. An exaggerated sense of responsibility for the actions of others
2. A tendency to confuse love and pity, with the tendency to "love" people they can pity and rescue

3. A tendency to do more than their share, all of the time
4. A tendency to become hurt when people don't recognize their efforts
5. An unhealthy dependence on relationships. The codependent will do anything to hold on to a relationship to avoid the feeling of abandonment
6. An extreme need for approval and recognition
7. A sense of guilt when asserting themselves
8. A compelling need to control others
9. Lack of trust in self and/or others
10. Fear of being abandoned or alone
11. Difficulty identifying feelings
12. Rigidity/difficulty adjusting to change
13. Problems with intimacy/boundaries
14. Chronic anger
15. Lying/dishonesty
16. Poor communications
17. Difficulty making decisions[5]

The spirit of Jezebel is looking for codependent personalities because they are passive, want to be liked, seek approval, doubt themselves, have a hard time saying no, and feel guilty when they can't live up to your expectations. These traits make a person easy prey for the Jezebel spirit to come in with its flattery and puffery to make you feel important and enlist you in its puppet show. If you see the characteristics listed above in your life, they are unhealthy at best and dangerous at worst. Work with the Holy Spirit to root these things out of your life by His grace and refuse to be Jezebel's puppet.

Breaking Jezebel and Ahab Curses

MHA also reports that codependency is a learned behavior that can be passed down from one generation to another. But I believe it can also be a spiritual issue related to a generational curse. Generational curses are found in several places in the Bible, and I believe Jezebel and Ahab curses are part of the mix.

A generational curse is just what it sounds like: a curse that passes down from generation to generation. There are many books written about generational curses. My goal here is not to offer a dissertation on the topic. But let's look at a few scriptures about generational curses so you can study this out in the Bible for yourself and understand the basics before we move forward:

> For I, the Lord your God, am a jealous God, visiting the iniquity of the fathers on the children to the third and fourth generation of them who hate Me.
>
> —Exodus 20:5–6

> By no means clear the guilty, visiting the iniquity of fathers on the children and on the children's children, to the third and the fourth generation.
>
> —Exodus 34:7

> The LORD is slow to anger and abounding in mercy, forgiving iniquity and transgression; but He will by no means clear the guilty, visiting the iniquity of the fathers upon the children to the third and fourth generation.
>
> —NUMBERS 14:18

> For I, the LORD your God, am a jealous God, visiting the iniquity of the fathers on the children, and on the third and fourth generations of those who hate Me.
>
> —DEUTERONOMY 5:9

As you can see, Scripture reveals that the impact of sin passes from generation to generation, hence the term *generational curse.* So it's not the sin that actually passes the bloodline, it's the curse that results from the sin—the penalty of sin. Larry Huch, senior pastor of New Beginnings, once put it to me this way:

> The world says it like this, "Like father, like son." The Word says it like this, "The iniquity of the father passes on from generation to generation." Many times we translate the word *iniquity* as "sin." But it's not the sin that passes on from generation to generation. It's the curse, the penalty. A curse is a spirit that passes from generation to generation until someone finally figures out how to stop it in Jesus's name.[6]

There are many takes on the so-called Jezebel curse and Ahab curse. Some point to dysfunctional families as the fruit of an Ahab curse or to Genesis 3:16 as the root of a Jezebel curse. The bottom line is that the penalty of sin can flow down a family line and someone has to rise up, repent, and break the curse in the name of Jesus. Ultimately only the Holy Spirit can show you if there is a curse operating in your life—or if you've fallen victim to Jezebel's or Ahab's agendas. But if you feel stirred in your spirit over this topic, I pray you'll cooperate with the Holy Spirit to explore it further.

Combatting Ahab Attacks Against Your Life

You may not be operating in an Ahab spirit—an Ahab spirit may be operating against you! You may think it's Jezebel working to trip you up, and it may very well be a Jezebel spirit that is front and center. But let's not forget that Ahab is often the instigator behind Jezebel's assignment. Remember Naboth's vineyard.

So how do you combat an Ahab attack against your life? First, you need to break any and all soul ties and common ground with Jezebel. The Bible doesn't use the term *soul tie*, but it is a biblical concept. A soul tie happens when people's souls are knit together in close relationships, like in the case of Jonathan and David (1 Sam. 18:1), during sexual relations when two become one flesh (Eph. 5:31), or when you make vows to or covenants with someone (Num. 30:2). Soul ties can be healthy with family, but they become unhealthy when sin—or evil spirits—are involved.

Practically speaking, having sex with someone—whether in or out of wedlock—can form a soul tie. Much the same, sharing personal information in confidence with a friend can create a soul tie, as can making a covenant with someone or pledging a vow of loyalty to them. You can even unknowingly make vows with spirits by saying things such as, "I'll never let anyone hurt me like that again," or "I will always protect my back from now on."

In fact, when you say such words, the spirit of Jezebel (and other spirits) hears you and sees it as an invitation to provide perverted protection by coming to your defense when you face unfair treatment. When you feel wronged, you may tend to manifest self-preserving behavior that's literally influenced by God's spiritual enemies. This is sinful in many ways, but mostly because we are supposed to trust in the Lord with all our hearts—not lean on our own understanding (Prov. 3:5) or lean on a demon power to protect us. If you have a soul tie with someone operating in a Jezebel or Ahab spirit, it is difficult to resist their influence in your life. You have to break the soul tie.

A soul tie is different from a curse, in that you entered into it willingly in most cases, even if it was unknowingly. The exception on the sexual front would be rape. People who are kidnapped often form soul ties with their captors, but these types of situations are not typical to most people. Again, most people enter into soul ties willfully, even if they don't realize it.

Breaking Soul Ties With Ahab and Jezebel

Often it's necessary to rid yourself of things in your possession connected with the one with whom you are breaking an ungodly soul tie. This could mean photographs, gifts, jewelry, clothing items—anything that ties you to that person. By the same token, if you've made any vows under your breath such as the ones I described—"I'll never let anyone hurt me again!"—repent of them right now. Even vows to people, such as, "I will never leave this church," or "I will love you to the end of time," need to be broken if they were spoken rashly or in the midst of a sinful relationship.

Breaking soul ties is not difficult, and it's similar to breaking a generational curse. It all starts with repentance. If you have committed some manner of sin that led you into a soul tie—usually that would mean sexual sin—renounce and repent of the offense to God's heart and ask for forgiveness. Receive that forgiveness, and then break the soul tie, in the name of Jesus!

Let me break that down a little more: you need to first renounce the soul tie and any vows you've made that were not of God. Next, you need to repent of entering into those soul ties or vows. Finally, you need to forgive any people involved in the soul ties or vows, forgive yourself, and receive God's forgiveness. Do all this out loud.

For example, "I renounce this soul tie with Jamie, in the name of Jesus. I want no part of this ungodly soul tie. I sever it right now and plead the blood of Jesus over my mind and mouth. I repent of the sin that led me into this soul tie. I forgive the ones I have tied myself to, I ask You to forgive them and me, and I forgive myself." You can elaborate on this phrase with more descriptors and sincerity, but these are the elements you need to address when breaking soul ties.

As far as eliminating common ground with these spiritual enemies, it's a similar process. It's difficult to resist an Ahab attack if you have common ground with Ahab that you aren't willing to let go of. The same applies to Jezebel or any other spirit. If you are finding yourself under constant attack, then it's possible you could have an open door for the enemy somewhere in your life. It's also just as possible that the devil is dead set on killing, stealing, and destroying your life. This is no time to play guessing games. Submit your heart to the Holy Spirit, examine yourself, and take the steps you need to take to get right with God or to receive His battle plans to overcome your spiritual enemies in this season.

In the next chapter we'll move on to spiritual enemies I call Jezebel's Yes-Men, and how this wicked spirit exploits false prophets in her demonic puppet show.

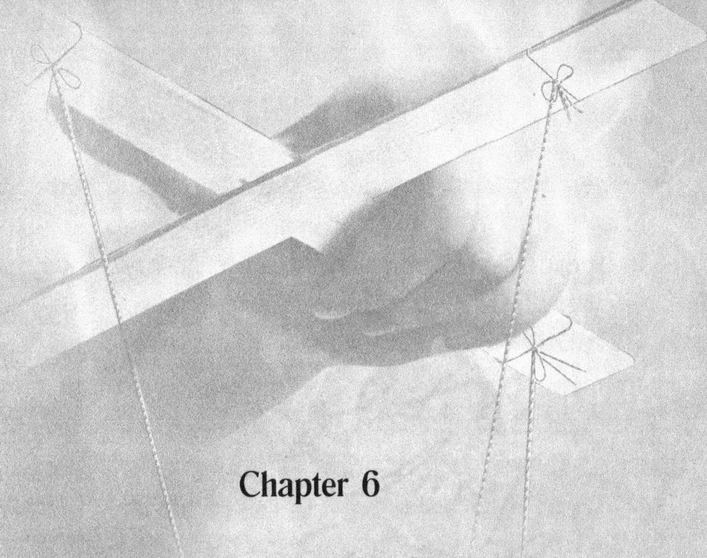

Chapter 6

JEZEBEL'S YES-MEN

APOSTLE DOUG LIKED to run a tight ship—and he liked to run it his way even if someone could show him a better way. Apostle Doug's ministry "ship" almost sank a few times. Many of the gospel projects for which he raised tens of thousands of dollars from his congregation failed within a year, and others were bearing little fruit. But he refused to shift course even when his prophetic yes-men were bailing water out of the boat.

A yes-man is someone who agrees with everything you say, for better or worse, to get your approval. *Merriam-Webster's Dictionary* defines *yes-man* as "a person who agrees with everything said; *especially*: one who endorses or supports without criticism every opinion or proposal of an associate or superior."[1] Ultimately, the only person who appreciates a yes-man is the one with whom the yes-man agrees. Everyone else sees them as pawns—or puppets—in the leader's hand.

Despite the piles of money sown into failed projects the Holy Spirit clearly did not inspire, no one dared suggest to Apostle Doug that he was missing the boat—much less God's will for his church. Anyone who dared speak up was marked a "religious spirit" or a "Jezebel spirit" and shunned. This stubborn apostle raised up an inner circle of prophetic yes-men he could trust to go along with whatever he plotted. In exchange for their blind loyalty Apostle Doug gave them authority to execute his vision, complete with superfluous religious titles, front row seats in service, and plenty of preaching opportunities. As far as the yes-men were concerned, Apostle Doug walked on water.

The buck stopped with Apostle Doug. He answered to no one—there was no accountability in his life—but everyone answered to him with a "yes." The only problem was the ministry "ships" kept sinking. In other words, the prophetic yes-men could prophesy prosperity and increase at church service after church service. The prophetic yes-men could share dreams and visions of success with the congregation week after week. But these prophetic yes-men weren't really speaking for God. They were prophesying the idolatry in Apostle Doug's heart. (See Ezekiel 14:4.)

Apostle Doug never admitted he missed God, and neither did his prophetic yes-men. Instead, they always blamed the shipwrecks and mishaps on spiritual warfare or people in the congregation who wouldn't get on board. He was never willing to admit that his idolatrous plans—and his methods—were the real issue. Of course, the prophetic yes-men would never tell Apostle Doug the truth because they wanted to keep their place in his apostolic kingdom. They knew the way to the top was telling Apostle Doug what he wanted to hear when he wanted to hear it—without exception.

It's not unusual to find yes-men in churches, businesses, and governments—and it's not a twenty-first century phenomenon. The carnal nature wants what it wants, and yes-men advance the cause. The Old Testament Queen Jezebel built a team of 850 prophetic yes-men around her who told her whatever she wanted to hear. These were the prophets of Baal and the prophets of Asherah. She let them eat at her table, which is a metaphor for feeding them from her kitchen. It was an intimate relationship, a high honor in the kingdom, and strong show of support within Israel for these prophetic puppets.

Remember, the true prophets—those who refused to become yes-men, those who dared speak what the Lord really was saying—were murdered or hidden in caves (1 Kings 18:4). Also remember that Israel was in a time of famine. By sustaining these false prophets with food and water, she was winning their hearts through their bellies. *Benson Commentary* says, "This sufficiently shows the infatuation and zeal of Jezebel for these idolatrous priests, that in a time of such famine she should take upon her to provide for eight hundred and fifty of them."[2]

Jezebel the False Prophetess

The 850 false prophets who ate at Jezebel's table became her puppets. The spirit that influenced Queen Jezebel—which we call the Jezebel spirit—is still using false prophets to forward its heinous agenda today, and this principality will become more prevalent in the end times. Consider the Jezebel Jesus calls out in the Book of Revelation and the connection to false prophets:

> But I have a few things against you: You permit that woman Jezebel, who calls herself a prophetess, to teach and seduce My servants to commit sexual immorality and eat food sacrificed to idols.
>
> —REVELATION 2:20

This woman Jezebel—who was influenced by the same spirit that tempted Queen Jezebel to murder the true prophets and support the false ones—called herself a prophetess. She was not a prophetess, but she called herself one, and her followers believed in her false prophetic utterances. They believed she was speaking for God.

Actually, *Jamieson-Fausset-Brown Bible Commentary* points out that the Hebrew word for *prophetess* in this scripture suggests Jesus was talking about more than one false prophetess—that He was calling out a set of false prophets that arose in the end times to teach and seduce His servants to commit sexual immorality and eat things sacrificed to idols.[3] Some commentators suggest this Jezebel could be symbolic of a false doctrine personified. In any case, there's a spirit behind this wickedness, and it uses the prophetic to win the hearts of men.

The spirit of Jezebel is an adulterous spirit and seduction is its goal. In Revelation 2:20 the word *seduce* comes from the Greek word *planaō*, which means "to cause to stray, to lead astray."[4] This is the same word that's used for the word *deceive* in 1 John 2:26: "I have written these things to you concerning those who deceive you." John was referring to antichrist spirits who deny the Father and the Son.

Ultimately, any spirit that opposes the will of Christ in the earth is an antichrist spirit, including the seducing spirit of Jezebel. But noteworthy is the truth that Jesus tied seduction to false prophecy in the last days in the King James Version of Mark 13:22: "For false Christs and false prophets shall rise, and shall shew signs and wonders, to seduce, if it were possible, even the elect." Other translations use the word *deceive* instead of seduce.

The word *deceive* or *seduce* in these translations comes from the Greek word *apoplanao*, which is a combination of two Greek words, *apo* and *planaō*. *Apo* speaks of a separation of a part from the whole, such as separating a believer from the body of Christ.[5] *Planaō*, as we just learned, means to cause to stray or lead astray. Here's the concept Jesus was trying to communicate: the enemy has to separate you from the truth before he can lead you into deception.

Seduction is a two-part process, and it happens slowly. Jezebel's seduction is a subtle one, and I am convinced that the Holy Spirit tries to warn this spirit's victims as they travel along the road to deception. I believe this because the Apostle John said by inspiration of the Holy Spirit that "the anointing which you have received from Him remains in you, and you do not need anyone to teach you. For as the same anointing teaches you concerning all things, and is truth, and is no lie, and just as it has taught you, remain in Him" (1 John 2:27). Ask the Lord right now to give you discernment to distinguish between the true and false prophetic.

Sexual Immorality: The False Teaching Connection

Remember Jesus said, "But I have a few things against you: You permit that woman Jezebel, who calls herself a prophetess, to teach and seduce My servants to commit sexual immorality and eat food sacrificed to idols" (Rev. 2:20). There's a clear connection between false doctrine and sexual immorality that can be traced all the way back to Queen Jezebel, but let's take a look at one major way this is manifesting in our generation. I call it the "gay Christian" or "gay-affirming Christian" movement.

Scripture is clear: you cannot practice homosexuality and claim Christ as Lord any more than you can mix oil and water. A separation always occurs. Homosexuals—who practice one manifestation of sexual immorality—are lumped in with the unrighteous, who will not inherit the kingdom of God, in 1 Corinthians 6:9–10: "Do not be deceived. Neither the sexually immoral, nor idolaters, nor adulterers, nor male prostitutes, nor homosexuals, nor thieves, nor covetous, nor drunkards, nor revilers, nor extortioners will inherit the kingdom of God" (Once again, the Greek word for *deceived* in this verse is *planaō*.)

Yet there's a rising movement of gays and gay-affirming Christians who are ignoring or twisting Scripture to form new—and false—doctrines that suggest God created homosexuals with same-sex attractions and the church needs to accept it, embrace it, and make room for the immorality in church leadership. In 2014 four denominations in less than seven days defied God's Word with clear support for gay marriage and/or gay clergy.

Young men such as Matthew Vines are publishing books such as *God and the Gay Christian* that mainstream media, professors of religion, liberal theologians, and others are praising as liberating for gays who have suffered in silence at the hand of the church. He has crafted a list of seven Bible-based reasons that support gay relationships, including excerpts from the Sermon on the Mount, claims that God destroyed Sodom and Gomorrah for its attitude toward the poor rather than its sexual immorality, and an argument that the Leviticus 18 ban on homosexual relationships is no longer valid because Christ fulfilled the Law.

Michael Brown, author of *Can You Be Gay and Christian?*, has this reaction to Vines's teaching: "Well, he is absolutely not representing the cause of Christ and is actively engaged in deceiving others, which puts him in a very serious category scripturally.... Without a doubt, he denies the authority of the Word and does not have a high view of Jesus or the Bible—that can be easily demonstrated. But has he ever known the Lord or has he crossed that line of apostasy yet? Only God knows right now."[6]

I believe the Jezebel spirit is one of the spirits working to propagate the lies that are holding gays—and others—in bondage to sexual immorality. Matthew Vines has become a de facto prophet for the movement in the twenty-first century, but we see a clear connection between false prophets and sexual immorality in the Bible. Beyond Queen Jezebel-sanctioned temple worship, during which prostitution, orgies, and homosexuality were prevalent, there's the false prophet Balaam.

Sexual Immorality and False Prophets

As I discuss in my book *A Prophet's Heart*, Bible historian Josephus tells the story of Balaam and Balak, the king of Moab who was hell-bent on finding a way to overcome Israel. Balak sent ambassadors to Balaam to entreat the prophet to come to them so that he would pronounce curses to destroy Israel. In Josephus's chronicle Balaam treats the ambassadors kindly and inquired of God to determine His will. Let's look at the story from the Bible itself:

> The elders of Moab and the elders of Midian went with the divination payments in their hand, and they came to Balaam and spoke to him the words of Balak. He said to them, "Lodge here tonight, and I will bring you word again, as the Lord will speak to me." And the leaders of Moab dwelt with Balaam. God came to Balaam and said, "Who are these men with you?"
>
> And Balaam said to God, "Balak the son of Zippor, king of Moab, has sent word to me, saying, 'A people went out of Egypt who covers the face of the earth. Now come, curse them for me. Perhaps I will be able to battle them and drive them out.'" God said to Balaam, "You will not go with them. You will not curse the people because they are blessed."
>
> —Numbers 22:7–12

Balaam's answer to the dignitaries who tempted him with riches was: "'Even if Balak were to give me his palace filled with silver and gold, I would be powerless to do anything against the will of the LORD my God. *But...*'" (Num. 22:18, NLT, emphasis added).

It was the word *but* that revealed Balaam's heart. God had already told him not to go with the Midianites and not to curse Israel. That should have settled the matter. But Balaam opened the case with the Lord again. The fact that Balaam was willing to go to God about the matter a second time—and the fact that he was talking about silver, gold, and palaces speaks volumes. Balaam had greed in his heart. He wanted to collect on Balak's offer.

The fact that he didn't collect makes no difference. His heart belied his allegiance to Jehovah. Although he could not curse Israel, he did find a way to lead them into sexual immorality. Balaam gave Balak a strategy that would cause the Israelites to essentially curse themselves. We see the strategy play out in Numbers 25, immediately after Balaam and Balak part ways in Numbers 24:

> Now Israel remained in Acacia Grove, and the people began to commit harlotry with the women of Moab. They invited the people to the sacrifices of their gods, and the people ate and bowed down to their gods. So Israel was joined to Baal of Peor, and the anger of the LORD was aroused against Israel. Then the LORD said to Moses, "Take all the leaders of the people and hang the offenders before the LORD, out in the sun, that the fierce anger of the LORD may turn away from Israel."
>
> —NUMBERS 25:1–4, NKJV

In Revelation 2:14, which is part of Jesus's letter to the church at Pergamos, we get confirmation that Balaam, the false prophet, was the one who incited the sexual immorality: "But I have a few things against you: You have there those who hold the teaching of Balaam, who taught Balak to cast a stumbling block before the children of Israel, to eat things sacrificed to idols and to commit sexual immorality."

That's the same accusation Jesus makes against Jezebel in Revelation 2:20: "But I have a few things against you: You permit that woman Jezebel, who calls herself a prophetess, to teach and seduce My servants to commit sexual immorality and eat food sacrificed to idols."

Balaam was influenced by the spirit of Jezebel—and so are many false prophets. Peter calls out false prophets in his second epistle to the church as those who seduce through heresy:

> But there were also false prophets among the people, just as there will be false teachers among you, who will secretly bring in destructive heresies, even denying the Lord who bought them, bringing swift destruction upon themselves. And many will follow their destructive ways, because of whom the way of truth will be blasphemed. And in their greed they will exploit you with deceptive words. Their judgment, made long ago, does not linger, and their destruction does not slumber.
>
> —2 PETER 2:1–3

Second Peter 2 is an eye-opening chapter about false prophets and false teachers. So is Jude, who talks about "dreamers" who defile the flesh (Jude 8) and specifically mentions Balaam among other depraved and doomed apostates (v. 11). These are sobering Scriptures and illustrate the fate of those who flow in a false prophetic spirit to forward Jezebel's agenda. But the Bible is also clear about their motive—money.

Remember, the false prophets ate at Queen Jezebel's table during a famine. In other words, they drew financial support from Jezebel. Peter shines light on Balaam, who loved the wages of wickedness (2 Pet. 2:15), and Jude calls out the error of Balaam as greed (Jude 11). We know that false prophets divine for money (Mic. 3:11). And we know that the love of money is a root of all evil (1 Tim. 6:10). Balaam was Balak's yes-man—and ultimately Jezebel's yes-man. Even when God would not allow him to flat-out curse the Israelites, his greedy heart still found a way to collect a reward.

Idolatrous False Prophets

Every person has his own weaknesses, and the spirit of Jezebel probes until it finds an open door to seduction—or until it determines there is no door. The three main areas of seduction are the lust of the flesh, the lust of the eyes, and the pride of life (1 John 2:16). Sexual immorality works through the lust of the flesh, which means we can't ultimately blame Jezebel for sexual sin or idolatry. The Jezebel spirit just taps into the carnal nature, but if we submit ourselves to God and resist Jezebel, it will flee (James 4:7).

Some false prophets hold true to sexual purity but blow it with idolatry. The lust of the eyes deals in the realm of idolatry. The lust of the eyes relates to covetousness—it wants what it sees—which the Bible connects to idolatry. Whether immorality or idolatry, the Holy Spirit commands us to put it to death: "Therefore put to death the parts of your earthly nature: sexual immorality, uncleanness, inordinate affection, evil desire, and covetousness, which is idolatry" (Col. 3:5).

False prophets often are marked by their own greed, but they also can tap into the idolatry in the heart of Jezebel's victims to seduce them. Let's look at how the Lord deals with people who hold idolatry in their hearts—and how this opens them up to Jezebel's deception:

> Then some of the elders of Israel came to me and sat before me. The word of the LORD came to me, saying: Son of man, these men have set up their idols in their heart and put the stumbling block of their iniquity before their face. Should I be inquired of by them at all?
>
> Therefore speak to them and say to them, Thus says the Lord GOD: Every man of the house of Israel who sets up his idols in his heart, and puts the stumbling block of his iniquity before his face, and comes to the prophet, I the LORD will answer him who comes according to the multitude of his idols, in order to seize the heart of the house of Israel who are estranged from Me through all their idols.
>
> Therefore say to the house of Israel, Thus says the Lord GOD: Repent and turn away from your idols and turn away your faces from all your abominations. For every one of the house of Israel or of the stranger who sojourns in Israel who separates himself from Me, and sets up his idols in his heart, and puts the stumbling block of his iniquity before his face, and comes to the prophet to inquire of Me for himself, I the LORD will answer him by Myself. And I will set My face against that man

> and will make him a sign and a proverb, and I will cut him off from the midst of My people. And you shall know that I am the LORD.
>
> —EZEKIEL 14:1–8

Doesn't that make you want to repent of idolatry right now? The stage is ripe for Jezebel's prophets to rise up and deceive, if it were possible, even the elect (Mark 13:22). Consider the words of the apostle Paul:

> Know this: In the last days perilous times will come. Men will be lovers of themselves, lovers of money, boastful, proud, blasphemers, disobedient to parents, unthankful, unholy, without natural affection, trucebreakers, slanderers, unrestrained, fierce, despisers of those who are good, traitors, reckless, conceited, lovers of pleasures more than lovers of God, having a form of godliness, but denying its power. Turn away from such people.
>
> —2 TIMOTHY 3:1–5

Paul also warned, "For the time will come when people will not endure sound doctrine, but they will gather to themselves teachers in accordance with their own desires, having itching ears" (2 Tim. 4:3).

We see some of this among congregations even now. Beyond universalism, there's the prosperity gospel that demonstrates only one side of the cross. There's the grace message that perverts the gospel. These are fables. Billy Graham once filled stadiums with his bold preaching on subjects such as hell and holiness. Today seeker-friendly preachers fill stadiums to hear a motivational message followed by a call to give. Many modern believers would cringe if they heard a classic Billy Graham sermon on hell. Again, some deny the existence of hell. We can't attribute all of this to Jezebel, but some of it falls right in this spirit's lap.

Jezebel's Destructive Doctrines

Beyond the gay-affirming Christian movement that is turning the leadership of some mainline Protestant denominations toward apostasy, there's also a hyper-grace—also called "distorted grace"—message that's seducing and deceiving believers in this hour. Jesus clearly warned His church against Jezebel's **false doctrines**, but this ancient evil has succeeded in hiding behind the mask of control and manipulation while few recognize its deeper agenda. Indeed, most do not see Jezebel as the propagator of false doctrines that give the saints a license to sin.

Despite the good works, love, service, faith, and patience of the church at Thyatira, Jesus had a few things against it because its leadership allowed a false prophetess named Jezebel to teach and seduce His servants to commit sexual immorality and idolatry (Rev. 2:20). Jesus said:

> I gave her time to repent of her sexual immorality, but she did not repent. Look! I will throw her onto a sickbed, and those who commit adultery with her into great tribulation, unless they repent of their deeds. I will put her children to death, and all the churches shall know that I am He who searches the hearts and minds. I will give to each one of you according to your deeds.
>
> —Revelation 2:21–23

Jesus went on to give an encouraging word to the rest of His church in Thyatira: "As many as do not have this teaching, who have not known what some call the 'depths of Satan,' I will put on you no other burden" (v. 24). That confirms Jezebel was guilty of teaching false doctrines. But for those who did not embrace Jezebel's false doctrine, Jesus encouraged them to "hold firmly what you have until I come" (v. 25). In other words, don't give in to this false doctrine—don't be deceived.

Some argue that the spirit of Jezebel does not exist because it is not named specifically in Scripture, but it's clear that the same demonic force was influencing both the Thyatira Jezebel and Old Testament Queen Jezebel. A study of Scripture shows the influence of this wicked spirit running from the Book of Genesis to the Book of Revelation. Suffice it to say that Jezebel has, for thousands of years, seduced God's servants, in part, with false assurances that God's grace is sufficient without repentance. The Bible clearly states that if we confess our sins, He is faithful and just to forgive us our sins and to cleanse us from all unrighteousness (1 John 1:9). But we have to confess our sin. When we sin, we also need to repent to maintain an intimate relationship with God.

The devil doesn't have any new tricks. The Jezebel spirit perverts God's Word, just as Satan did when he tempted Jesus in the wilderness. Satan told Jesus:

> If You are the Son of God, throw Yourself down. For it is written, "He shall give His angels charge concerning you," and "In their hands they shall lift you up, lest at any time you dash your foot against

> a stone." Jesus said to him, "It is also written, 'You shall not tempt the Lord your God.'"
>
> —MATTHEW 4:6–7

Satan also tried to get Jesus to idolize him, and Jesus told Him, "You shall worship the Lord your God, and Him only shall you serve'" (v. 10).

Much the same, Jezebel works to seduce you into sin by twisting Scripture. Jezebel's teachings give you a license to commit immorality and idolatry. Jezebel will tell you that it's OK to fornicate if you love another person because it doesn't violate the one new commandment Jesus gave us (John 13:34). Jezebel will set you up to idolize your favorite preacher, possibly while working behind the scenes to seduce him into sexual immorality.

Much of the church is so fascinated with this demonic rock star's mask of control and manipulation that it misses the subtle deceptive doctrines. And much of the church denies the existence of the Jezebel spirit. Jezebel is like the Lady of Kingdoms whom no one sees. (See Isaiah 47, NKJV.) But the Jezebel deception is slowly eroding as spiritually discerning saints begin to see behind the mask of control and manipulation to the deeper agenda—false doctrines that pave a highway to God's judgment.

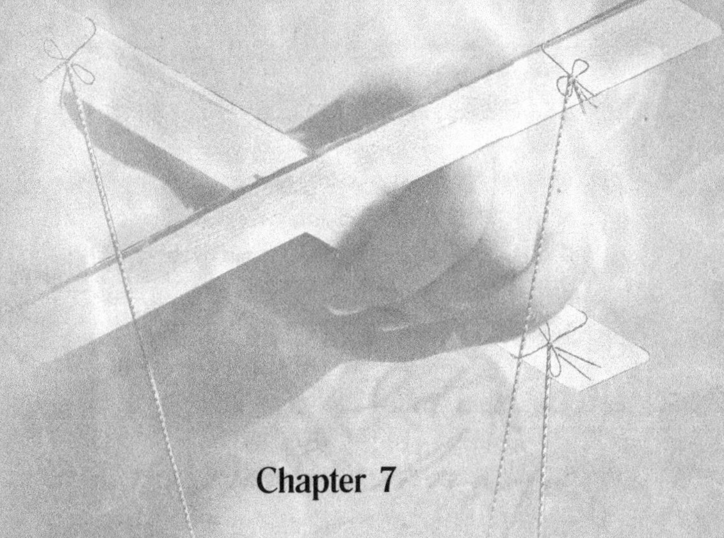

Chapter 7

CONFRONTING JEZEBEL'S FALSE PROPHETS

GIVING THEIR SON a name such as "God is Jehovah," Elijah's parents must have had high hopes for him. I can imagine Elijah's dad sharing with him the account of God's creating Adam and Eve; how they fell from grace; how Cain murdered his brother, Abel; how Noah built an ark that preserved humanity; how God made a covenant with Abraham; and how Moses delivered the Israelites out of Pharaoh's bondage.

Elijah's little prophetic ears must have perked up when his dad told him the story of how God called Moses and sent him to confront mighty Pharaoh. It turned into a showdown between men carrying the true power of God and magicians working false signs and wonders. It was a scene that would certainly inspire awe in a young prophet's heart. Let's listen in:

> Now the LORD spoke to Moses and to Aaron, saying, "When Pharaoh shall speak to you, saying, 'Show a miracle,' then you shall say to Aaron, 'Take your rod, and throw it before Pharaoh,' and it shall become a serpent."
>
> So Moses and Aaron went to Pharaoh, and they did what the LORD had commanded. And Aaron threw down his rod before Pharaoh and before his servants, and it became a serpent. Then Pharaoh also called the wise men and the sorcerers. Then the magicians of Egypt likewise performed with their secret arts. For every man threw down his rod, and they became serpents. But Aaron's rod swallowed up their rods. Nonetheless, Pharaoh's heart hardened so that he would not listen to them, just as the LORD had said.
>
> —EXODUS 7:8–13

I can just imagine Elijah cheering blow by blow as God showed Himself mighty for Aaron and Moses time after time until the ultimate blow was struck and Aaron's rod swallowed up the magicians' rods. Pharaoh's magicians were put to shame, and Jehovah God, the one from whom Elijah took his name, was glorified. What confidence this must have inspired in the young prophet!

WILL THE REAL GOD PLEASE STAND UP?

Surely the memory of Aaron's victorious showdown with false powers stayed with Elijah right up until the day he confronted the false prophets of Baal and Asherah. When God told Elijah to gather all Israel on Mount Carmel, along with the 450 prophets of Baal and 400 prophets of Asherah who ate at Jezebel's table, there was never a shred of doubt in his mind as to how the showdown would play out.

Allow me to set the stage. Elijah called for the showdown, and Ahab quickly obliged. He called all the children of Israel and gathered the false prophets at Mount Carmel. Jezebel didn't show up for the showdown. It's possible, though unlikely, that she didn't know about the fierce face-off. Only God knows what Ahab expected, but it's clear that Elijah expected nothing less than total victory in the name of his God:

> Elijah came to all the people and said, "How long will you stay between two opinions? If the LORD is God, follow Him, but if Baal, then follow him." And the people did not say a word.
>
> —1 KINGS 18:21

The fact that Israel remained silent shows the sad state of the nation. They weren't even willing to fake allegiance to Jehovah. This must have grieved Elijah—and Jehovah—but the prophet was not shaken. Elijah set out the terms of the showdown. He asked for two bulls and gave the false prophets first dibs on which bull they wanted to sacrifice to their gods. Each would cut the bull into pieces and lay it on some wood but leave the fire out of the sacrificial equation. The false prophets would cry out to their gods, and Elijah would cry out to Jehovah. The God who answered by fire would win the contest.

The brazen, willful false prophets agreed to the terms. Clearly they were deceived, just as false prophets today are deceived. They never would have gone through with the showdown if they hadn't thought they would win.

They were as confident in their false gods as Elijah was in his true God. The Bible says the false prophets called on the name of Baal from morning until noontime. Of course, there was no answer. When the crying out didn't work, they started leaping around the altar. When the leaping didn't work, they cried aloud some more and starting cutting themselves with knives and lances until they bled. And when that didn't work, they started uttering false prophecies until nighttime. And, of course, that didn't work either. (See 1 Kings 18:25–29.)

Going Toe to Toe With False Prophets

I can imagine the false prophets were worn out from leaping, their throats sore from crying out, and their bodies aching from self-mutilation. They finally gave up and let Elijah take his turn. The first thing Elijah did was to repair the altar of the Lord that was broken down. He took twelve stones representing the number of the tribes of Israel and built an altar. What happened next was even more impressive than the story Elijah's dad (probably) told him about Aaron's rod and the magicians:

> And he built an altar in the name of the Lord with stones, and he made a trench around the altar, so deep that it could contain two seahs of seed. He arranged the wood and cut the bull in pieces and laid him on the wood and said, "Fill four barrels with water, and pour it on the burnt sacrifice and on the wood." He said, "Do it a second time," and they did it a second time. And he said, "Do it a third time," and they did it the third time. The

> water ran all around the altar and also filled the trench with water.
>
> At the time of the offering of the evening sacrifice, Elijah the prophet came near and said, "The LORD, God of Abraham, Isaac, and of Israel, let it be known this day that You are God in Israel and that I am Your servant and that I have done all these things at Your word. Hear me, O LORD, hear me, so that this people may know that You are the LORD God and that You have turned their hearts back again."
>
> Then the fire of the LORD fell and consumed the burnt sacrifice and the wood and the stones and the dust and licked up the water that was in the trench. When all the people saw it, they fell on their faces and said, "The LORD, He is God! The LORD, He is God!" Elijah said to them, "Arrest the prophets of Baal, and do not let one of them escape." And they arrested them, and Elijah brought them down to the Kishon brook and executed them there.
>
> —1 KINGS 18:32–40

WARRING AGAINST FALSE DOCTRINE

Elijah rid the land of Jezebel's prophets in his day, but the same spirits that influenced those false prophets have crept into the modern church. We aren't called to execute them, but there are times when the Holy Spirit will lead us to confront error—or at least refuse to sit in a church where Jezebel's influence is dominating the atmosphere.

I believe the Holy Spirit tries to warn us about false doctrines circulating in our midst, but if we choose to embrace these teachings for any reason—whether they indirectly justify our sin, faintly feed our idolatry, or otherwise subtly seduce us away from the living Word of God—He eventually will let us embrace the lie. God's Spirit leads us and guides us into all truth (John 16:13), but if we willfully reject His leading, His guidance, and His truth, He will leave us to our will. Indeed, Paul warned Timothy that "the Spirit clearly says that in the last times some will depart from the faith and pay attention to seducing spirits and doctrines of devils, speaking lies in hypocrisy, having their consciences seared with a hot iron" (1 Tim. 4:1–2).

So, again, we're not called to execute false prophets, false teachers, and false apostles with the edge of the sword. But we are called to wield the sword of the Spirit, which is the Word of God, in the face of any doctrine or teaching that tries to seduce us away from the truth. Of course, Jezebel will war against those who war against false doctrine. Consider the backlash against Elijah as an example:

> And Ahab told Jezebel all that Elijah had done and how he had executed all the prophets with the sword. Then Jezebel sent a messenger to Elijah, saying, "So let the gods do to me and more also, if I do not make your life as the life of one of them by tomorrow about this time." When he saw that she was serious, he arose and ran for his life to Beersheba, which belongs to Judah, and left his servant there. But he went a day's journey into the wilderness and came and sat down under a juniper tree and asked that he might die, saying, "It is enough! Now, O LORD, take my life, for I am not better than my fathers."
>
> —1 KINGS 19:1–4

When you start throwing golden calves into the fire—that is, when you expose false doctrines, false gods, destructive heresies, false prophecies, and anything else that perverts or opposes the Word of God—some people start gnashing their teeth at you. People are going to start releasing fearful word curses at you. Don't let that stop you from throwing golden calves into the fire, but please remember we're not wrestling against flesh and blood as Elijah did. We're wrestling against "principalities, against powers, against the rulers of the darkness of this world, and against spiritual forces of evil in the heavenly places" (Eph. 6:12).

Thou Shalt Not Judge?

One of the most common outcries against calling out false doctrines insists, "Thou shalt not judge." That's actually not one of the Ten Commandments Moses brought down from Sinai when he found the Israelites worshipping Baal and got so angry that he took the golden calf they had made, burned it, ground it to powder, scattered it on the water, and made the children of Israel drink it (Exod. 32:19–20).

"Thou shalt not judge" isn't actually in the Bible. Jesus did say, "Judge not, that you be not judged" (Matt. 7:1), but this was in the context of the Sermon on the Mount lifestyle. Jesus was talking about judging your brother in a wrong spirit. He actually went on to say that we should judge—but not until we deal with our own hearts (the planks in our eyes). We have to speak the truth in love. Sometimes the truth sounds harsh to someone in deception or sin. But our motive is never to cut. Our motive is always to heal.

Jesus also said, "Do not judge according to appearance, but judge with righteous judgment" (John 7:24, NKJV). What is a "righteous" judgment? Jesus's interaction with the Pharisees is a good example. Some things look spiritual. Some things smell holy. Some things sound godly. Like the Pharisees. But the Pharisees, as a group, were among those Jesus judged most harshly—even pronouncing woes on some of them! In fact, Jesus did more judging than any other figure we find in Scripture. His motive in judging is to expose the sin and deliver people from evil. Again, that should be our motive in judging.

Think about it for a minute. Let's say there's a patient sitting in a doctor's office awaiting test results from a biopsy. The results clearly show that cancer is killing him, but the doctor doesn't want to point out anything negative so he tells the patient everything looks fine and sends him on his merry way. The cancer progresses, and the patient dies. That's called malpractice. It's also called carelessness. The doctor didn't care enough about his patient to tell him the truth. That's not love.

Jesus Didn't Tolerate False Doctrine

It's the same way with righteous judgment. When we judge in the spirit of Christ, we are obeying Jesus. We are pointing out the cancer. Exposing error in the church is an expression of Christ's love and grace. We are sounding the alarm so that people can turn and run in the other direction. Jesus commended the church of Ephesus for calling out the false apostles (Rev. 2:2) and rebuked the church at Thyatira for tolerating a false prophetess called Jezebel (v. 20).

Making a righteous judgment is not about judging ministries whose styles you disagree with. Making a righteous judgment is not about finding a point of contention over a small difference in interpretation—such as the timing of the Rapture or even the infilling of the Holy Spirit—and trying to mark someone as a heretic. Making a righteous judgment deals with flat-out sin or false doctrine that is leading people away from the truth.

Jesus didn't preach a message of tolerance for false doctrine, nor did John, Paul, Peter, or Jude. Paul said he would continue to "cut off the opportunity from those who desire an opportunity to be found equal to us in what they boast about. For such are false apostles and deceitful workers, disguising themselves as apostles of Christ" (2 Cor. 11:12–13).

Paul also taught Titus to do the same, noting "there are many unruly men, empty talkers and deceivers, especially those of the circumcision, who must be silenced, who subvert whole houses by teaching for dishonest gain things they ought not teach. One of them, a prophet of their own, said, 'The Cretans are always liars, evil beasts, and idle gluttons!' This witness is true. So rebuke them sharply that they may be sound in the faith" (Titus 1:10-13). Paul also taught Titus: "Speak these things, exhort, and rebuke with all authority. Let no one despise you" (Titus 2:15, NKJV).

We must remain loyal to Jesus. That means we must remain true to the Word of God. We must abide by the doctrines of Christ. We must be faithful witnesses in this generation. We must sound the alarm, hoping and praying that the ones who preach false doctrines will repent and the ones who have bought into false doctrines will find deliverance. We must make a righteous judgment. In order to do that, we must be students of the Word and sensitive to the Holy Spirit.

Just as Jesus prophesied, false prophets and false teachers are rising. Many will be deceived. The love of many will grow cold. And many will fall away. As much as we want unity, we can't compromise truth for the sake of unity. That's really not unity at all. We cannot stand by—like a physician who doesn't want to tell his patient she has cancer because he wants to stay positive—while so many in the body of Christ worship another Jesus centered on a different gospel. That, my friends, is not love, and it's not biblical.

Don't Fall Into Heresy Hunting

I won't take part in it—and I implore you not to take part in it either. If you are listening to teachers on TV who aren't preaching the unadulterated Word of God, turn it off. If you are sitting in a church where Jezebel's influence is working, ask the Holy Spirit what to do. He may have you leave or stay there and pray for a season, but guard your heart from the deception. I've known some who claimed the Holy Spirit told them to stay in a deceived church to intercede—only to wind up deceived themselves.

That said, you don't want to go on a witch hunt, either. You don't want to become one of those nasty heresy hunters who work to make a name for themselves on the Internet. There's a huge difference between discerning a spirit of error that keeps people from a full understanding of Jesus and accusing people of full-blown **heresy** that keeps people from receiving salvation. Even though deception is running rampant in the body of Christ, I shun the work of **heresy hunters** who have made it their mission to discredit anyone and everyone who has a theology with which they find some small point of contention.

When it comes to **heresy,** we expose it and refuse to fellowship with those propagating it. But even then we don't chase them down and persecute them. We pray that God will break in with light and expose the darkness that has clouded their minds. To take any other approach is simply a wrong spirit that could ultimately lead you into a deeper deception than the one you believe they are exposing.

How to Expose Jezebel's Prophets and Teachers

The Bible admonishes us to try the spirits. John the apostle said, "Beloved, do not believe every spirit, but test the spirits to see whether they are from God, because many false prophets have gone out into the world" (1 John 4:1). We're also called to mark those who cause divisions among us contrary to sound doctrine—and avoid them (Rom. 16:17).

Paul told Titus to rebuke those who are insubordinate, idle talkers, deceivers—their mouths needed to be stopped because they taught untruths for greedy gain. We're supposed to reject a divisive man after the first and second admonition (Titus 3:10). We're not supposed to fellowship with the unfruitful works of darkness—but reprove them (Eph. 5:11), withdraw from them (2 Thess. 3:6), and turn away from them (2 Tim. 3:5–7).

So how exactly do you expose—or confront—Jezebel's prophets and teachers? Do you publicly name their names, or do you just leave their congregations? Do you try to set up a meeting with them to speak the truth in love, or do you run the other way and not look back? Do you warn people with whom you are in close relationship, or do you keep your mouth shut and let the Holy Spirit deal with it?

There's no single answer to this question. Like the flight attendants always say when they go over instructions for a plane crash: put the oxygen mask on your face first and then help others put on their masks. In other words, you first have to free yourself from the influence of Jezebel's prophets and teachers before you can even think of helping anybody else. Helping may mean naming names, or it may be interceding for those under the influence of Jezebel's deceptive prophets and teachers.

I can't give you a blanket formula, but I can offer you some biblical examples on how to deal with this difficult issue. As you read on, remember that anything you do needs to be done with the right spirit and the right motive. No matter how much harm a deceived preacher is causing, you still need to be harmless as a dove in your approach. You need the Holy Spirit's discernment and wisdom—and "the wisdom that is from above is first pure, then peaceable, gentle, open to reason, full of mercy and good fruits, without partiality, and without hypocrisy" (James 3:17). Our heart should always be to reconcile people to the truth, not embitter them toward us.

How the Apostles Handled Exposing the False Prophets

There's a time to name names and a time not to name names. Who were the men "who secretly crept in, who were marked long ago for this condemnation... [who] are ungodly men, who pervert the grace of our God into immorality," whom Jude talked about in his letter to the church (vv. 4–5)? Who were the ones Jude pronounced woe on—the ones who went the way of Cain, ran greedily in the error of Balaam for profit, and perished in the rebellion of Korah (v. 11)? Who were the "spots" in the love feasts (v. 12)? You can't tell me because Jude never named them.

What about the false teachers Peter pointed out? He called these depraved false teachers "spots and blemishes" who were "carousing in their own deceptions," having "eyes full of adultery and that cannot cease from sin, enticing unstable souls"; he called them out for having hearts "trained in covetous practices"; he called them "accursed children" (2 Pet. 2:13–14, NKJV). He marked them as those who "have forsaken the right way and gone astray, following the way of Balaam the son of Beor, who loved the wages of unrighteousness" (v. 15, NKJV). And he called them out for promising liberty when they themselves were "slaves of corruption" (v. 19, NKJV). Tell me, who were they? You can't tell me because Peter never named them.

And let's not forget the false apostles Paul pegged. He called these false apostles "deceitful workers, transforming themselves into the apostles of Christ" (2 Cor. 11:13, NKJV)

And then he dared to say that it was no wonder, since Satan himself transforms into an angel of light. Paul went on to say that it's no great thing if Satan's ministers, these false apostles, "also transform themselves into ministers of righteousness, whose end will be according to their works" (vv. 13–15, NKJV). Tell me, who were they? You can't tell me because Paul never named them.

There is a time to name names, and there is a time not to name names. Paul named Phygellus and Hermogenes as ones who turned away from him (2 Tim. 1:15). He also named Demas, who forsook him because he "loved this present world" (2 Tim. 4:10). But keep in mind that these instances were in a personal letter warning his spiritual son rather than in a letter to the entire body of Christ warning of false gospels. That doesn't mean there's never a time for a leader to write an open letter to the body of Christ about someone who is in error, but the Holy Spirit must guide the leader in doing that, and the person must handle it in a spirit that seeks reconciliation rather than condemnation.

John named Diotrephes in a letter to the local church at Gaius. He said: "Diotrephes, who loves to put himself first among them, did not accept us. Because of this, if I come, I will bring up what kinds of works he does: ranting against us with malicious words. Not content with that, he does not accept the brothers, and stops those who want to, and throws them out of the church" (3 John 9–10). But keep in mind that John wrote this from a disciplinary stance to that single church body, not as a warning to the universal church about false gospels.

Jesus issued warning after warning about false

prophets and false teachers and false Christs—and wrong doctrine. We don't know the names of the ones He was warning about. He often shared the principles these false ones taught—but not always. For example, He didn't tell us what doctrines the false Christs and false prophets who will rise and show signs and wonders to deceive would be propagating (Mark 13:22). He told us so we could be ready and discerning.

When Jesus pronounced woe on the scribes, Pharisees, and hypocrites, He explained why they were worthy of woe, but He didn't follow up His list of woes with a list of names. (See Matthew 23.) He clearly outlined the reasons for the woes, but that doesn't automatically paint every Pharisee with the brush of guilt. Jesus called out Satan by name, but He wasn't in the habit of calling out specific people. I believe that's because Satan is the one influencing the false prophets, false teachers, false Christs, and wrong doctrine. We're not wrestling against flesh and blood but against "principalities, against powers, against the rulers of the darkness of this world, and against spiritual forces of evil in the heavenly places" (Eph. 6:12).

Always Follow the Holy Spirit

So, why did those who scribed the Bible choose to name names at some times and not at other times? Could it be possible they were led by the Holy Spirit? If the Scripture is Spirit-inspired, and it is, then these men were led at times to name names and at other times not to name names.

The same holds true today. I've named names and been criticized for it. I've declined to name names and been criticized for it. I've named names and been thanked for it. It makes no difference to me. I'm not here to win man's approval. I've been delivered from the man-pleasing spirit. I'm here to obey God.

It's the fear of the Lord that drives me to write warnings. I'm staying true to my prophetic calling. These warnings coming through my pen—and the pen of many others—are not what is bringing division to the body. Rather, the people preaching error (or not living right) are causing the controversy and bringing the division. When we expose the error, we are pointing people back to Jesus and toward true unity.

I refuse to stand by and watch a cancer grow in the body and then turn a blind eye as many are led astray. I refuse to whitewash a false gospel in the name of unity. That's called "compromise," and there's a price to pay for taking that route. I'm willing to pay the price for standing for truth. I don't want to pay the price for compromising God's calling on my life. Do you? Think of Elijah. Think of Paul. Think of Jesus. If you run into one of Jezebel's false prophets, don't rise up in the flesh but pray in the Spirit. He will show you what to do and in what timing to do it.

In the next chapter we'll take a closer look at another group of puppets in Jezebel's show: the eunuchs.

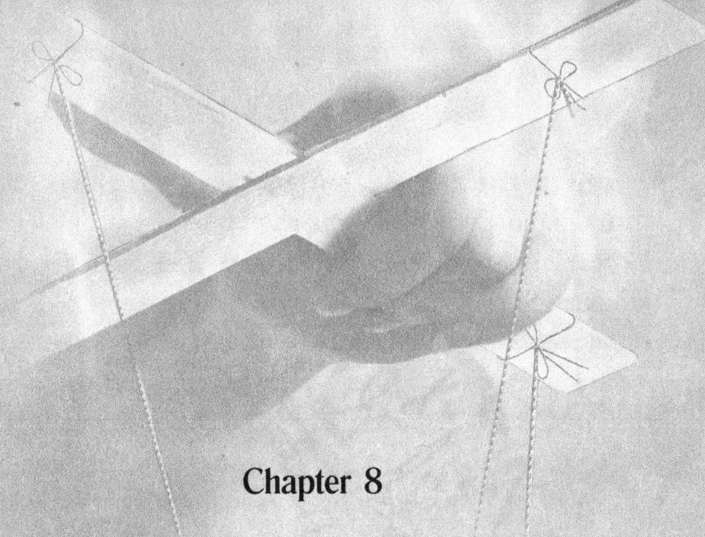

Chapter 8

THE ROYAL EUNUCHS

MINDY HAD SUFFERED abuse most of her life. Her mom abandoned the family on the day she was born. She was raised in a "never enough to go around" atmosphere with older siblings who blamed her for their mom's bailing out. When Mindy grew up, her boyfriend manipulated her into performing sexual acts that violated her conscience and left her feeling ashamed. Mindy thought things would be different after she surrendered her life to Christ and joined a church. Unfortunately it didn't turn out that way. Jezebel was waiting to pounce on her wounded soul—but I'm getting ahead of myself.

When Mindy entered the kingdom of God, she had one desire: to love the Lord with all her heart, all her soul, all her strength, and all her mind—and to serve Him all the days of her life. It took Mindy years to find a church in which she felt comfortable—and, in fact, she was churchless for about a year after one pastor offered "hurtful advice" about a personal issue she was wading through. Finally, she found a church with a strong leader, Pastor Jake, who built her up and embraced her gifts. Finally, she thought, people were willing to allow her to serve without diving into her painful past.

Still a baby Christian, she was ignorant of Satan's devices (2 Cor. 2:11) and never suspected that this strong, charismatic leader had misguided motives to use her gifts and talents to build his personal ministry kingdom rather than the kingdom of God. She was so hungry to share her gifts and talents in the church that she never felt Jezebel's hands wrapping around her throat. No, she never dreamed that this determined pastor would misuse his spiritual authority to make her a eunuch.

Mindy was not equipped to resist the enemy on the battleground onto which she had unknowingly walked. She had never heard of principalities and powers such as Jezebel and wasn't familiar with the concept of eunuchs. Even when she learned about spiritual warfare she was still clueless that the pastor was under the influence of a Jezebel spirit that had made her—and many others—loyal eunuchs in his royal kingdom.

Mindy was deceived, partly by her longing to find acceptance from a father figure she never had—but there was another factor in place. The hurts and wounds had stripped Mindy of her self-esteem. Pastor Jake offered Mindy delegated authority to get his dirty work done in the church. Mindy truly thought she was serving the Lord. She liked the way it made her feel. She thought she was laying down her life for Christ, but she was really laying down her life for a Jezebelic pastor who paid her in the currency she valued most: power. Mindy manipulated church members to follow Pastor Jake's will, delivered harsh corrective words when they wouldn't, and even made fearful threats on his behalf. She was unknowingly advancing Jezebel's wicked agenda.

Ironically, Mindy was absolutely convinced she was being submissive and that those who would not pick up their crosses and blindly follow Pastor Jake were in rebellion to Jesus. Being in the "inner circle" and knowing everybody's personal business made Mindy feel important. Instead of love building her up, knowledge puffed her up (1 Cor. 8:1, NKJV). She relished working closely with Pastor Jake—so closely, in fact, that accusations came that she was having an affair with him. Mindy never knew Jezebel had made her a eunuch and that she was suffering spiritual abuse—or that she was helping this wicked spirit make eunuchs of others.

Why Jezebel Needs Eunuchs

Remember, Jezebel's false kingdom infrastructure relies on eunuchs. A "eunuch" is a man who has been castrated, usually before puberty. The word *eunuch* comes from the Hebrew word *caric*, which means "to castrate."[1] Although Jesus made it clear that some eunuchs made a conscious decision to become eunuchs out of their own free will for the kingdom of God's sake (Matt. 19:12), Jezebel's modern-day spiritual eunuchs don't fall into this category. Jezebel is on a mission to spiritually castrate the saints and keep them under its thumb.

But why does Jezebel need eunuchs? How do these eunuchs fit into Jezebel's wicked plot? What role, specifically, do eunuchs play in Jezebel's puppet show? Jezebel uses eunuchs to do its bidding. For example, eunuchs in Queen Jezebel's royal bedchambers did not have the luxury of deciding what tasks they would or would not perform. The eunuchs were her servants and did her bidding without question, though probably begrudgingly at times. Eunuchs perform tasks that Jezebel does not want to do or cannot do itself.

Nevertheless, Jezebel's eunuchs play a key role in forwarding this spirit's master plot. Eunuchs are Jezebel's servants. It may have been a eunuch that delivered the fearful curse to Elijah that sent him running into the wilderness, hoping to die, after defeating the false prophets at Mount Carmel. Motivated by fear or a need for acceptance, Jezebel's spiritual eunuchs are at her beck and call.

Eunuchs are essentially Jezebel's spiritual slaves. So what types of tasks do spiritual eunuchs perform? Although some like to make suppositions about eunuchs that are extra-biblical at best—including suggestions that eunuchs guard Jezebel—I find it dangerous to stray too far from what we see in the Bible with regard to the historical role of eunuchs.

It's dangerous, I believe, to get too overly specific about all the ways Jezebel used eunuchs because Scripture doesn't offer those details. We don't see eunuchs carrying Jezebel's armor, for example, or spying on people Jezebel was targeting for destruction. With regard in particular to eunuchs guarding Jezebel, we know that's not necessarily accurate, considering that the eunuchs were not loyal to Jezebel in the end—they threw her down at Jehu's call (2 Kings 9:33). We can draw out examples from Scripture, but no one has all the answers.

My point is this: straying too far from what the Word reveals about Jezebel's eunuchs can open the door to false accusations that hurt the saints and leave real eunuchs in bondage. That said, I do believe that Jezebel uses eunuchs as messengers—and I believe there are two examples in Scripture where Jezebel used eunuchs to deliver messages to forward her agenda. I am also convinced this principle applies to how the spirit of Jezebel operates.

Jezebel's Messengers

A key role eunuchs play in Jezebel's puppet show is that of messenger. Although the Bible does not explicitly say that eunuchs delivered messages on Jezebel's behalf, I believe they were the messengers who helped this spirit murder Naboth and release fear in the heart of the prophet Elijah. It is also possible that the eunuchs played a role in having the prophets massacred. The Bible says, "Jezebel massacred the prophets of the Lord" (1 Kings 18:4, NKJV), but we know that Queen Jezebel herself did not strike them down with a sword. Eunuchs may have delivered the message to Jezebel's soldiers without Ahab's knowledge.

We know, in any case, that Queen Jezebel had Naboth murdered without Ahab's knowledge. As we discussed in chapter 4, Ahab wanted Naboth's vineyard so he could grow a vegetable garden next to his house. He offered Naboth what he considered a better vineyard or, if Naboth preferred, a cash payment. But Naboth refused. That spiraled Ahab into a state of depression, and he wouldn't get out of bed or eat. When Jezebel found him in this state, she asked him what was the matter, and he told her. Then she said to him:

> "Are you not the governor of the kingdom of Israel? Get up and eat bread, and let your heart be happy, for I will get the vineyard of Naboth the Jezreelite for you." So she wrote letters in Ahab's name and sealed them with his seal and sent the letters to the elders and to the nobles that were in the city where Naboth lived. In the letters she wrote, "Proclaim a fast, and set Naboth on high among the people, and set two men, sons of Belial, before him, to bear witness against him, saying, 'You blasphemed God and the king.' And then carry him out and stone him, so that he will die."
>
> —1 KINGS 21:7–10

I believe Jezebel sent her eunuch to deliver that message. It worked. The message was delivered. Naboth was murdered. Ahab got his field. I also believe Queen Jezebel sent a eunuch to deliver her fearful message to Elijah. As I write in my book *Satan's Deadly Trio*:

> Jezebel released a word curse against Elijah that carried a spirit of fear when she sent him this message: "So let the gods do to me, and more also, if I make not thy life as the life of one of them by tomorrow about this time" (1 Kings 19:2, KJV). This word curse released witchcraft imaginations against Elijah's mind. The Bible says, "And when he *saw* that, he arose he arose and ran for his life, and went to Beersheba, which belongs to Judah,

and left his servant there" (1 Kings 19:3, NKJV; emphasis mine).

Elijah *saw* something when Jezebel released her witchcraft against him. Elijah imagined her words coming to pass—he imagined the curse as true. Maybe you can relate to witchcraft imaginations that are released at your mind through word curses. God gave us a holy imagination to use for His glory. But Scripture repeatedly reveals that man uses his imagination for evil (see Gen. 6:5; Prov. 6:18; Jer. 3:17; Luke 1:51). Our unrenewed mind's propensity to meditate on what is not good is to witchcraft's advantage.

As holy as Elijah was, and despite his powerful anointing, Jezebel's witchcraft sent him running for his life. By leaving his servant behind, he effectively isolated himself from those who could speak truth into his life—another tactic of Jezebel. The mighty Elijah actually sat down under a broom tree and prayed that he would die: "It is enough! Now, LORD, take my life, for I am no better than my fathers!" (1 Kings 19:4, NKJV). Then he went to sleep. Elijah took a long nap, woke up just to eat, and went right back to bed! All this after Jezebel released a word curse against him that set his imagination—and his feet—running into the wilderness.[2]

The Power of Life and Death

The Bible speaks about Jezebel and her witchcraft (2 Kings 9:22). We've already identified that Jezebel operates in a false spiritual authority, committing murder by using

Ahab's signet ring to order Naboth's execution. Today I believe the spirit of Jezebel works its witchcraft in large part through the power of death and life that are in our tongues (Prov. 18:21). The witchcraft Jezebel was practicing—the witchcraft Jehu called out in 2 Kings 9:22—comes from the Hebrew word *kesheph*, which is related to sorcery and includes casting spells. In charismatic circles we'd call Jezebel's threat to Elijah a *word curse.*

Witchcraft is a spiritual force that I believe operates with or without the power of death and life that is in our tongues. But words of death are one of the fastest ways Jezebel's messengers get the job done because it takes the battle out of the realm of the imagination and makes it real. Elijah, for example, may have wondered what Jezebel would do when she found out he killed all her false prophets. But he didn't start running away or wishing he was dead until after Jezebel's messenger released word curses at him.

I've never had anyone release witchcraft at me unto death, but I have had many release spiritual witchcraft through their lips, and I can attest to the spiritual force that is attached to those words. Some have suggested that I will rot in hell for my biblical stand against homosexuality, for instance; while others have verbally attacked me for speaking out against false prophets who merchandise the saints. Of course, both homosexuality and false prophets have spiritual ties to Jezebel. I talk more about the power of witchcraft in my book *Satan's Deadly Trio.*

Jezebel's spiritual eunuchs—Christians in bondage to the demonic pressure that comes from this principality—are violating Scripture in more ways than one. The Bible says, for example, "Let no corrupt word proceed out of your mouth, but what is good for necessary edification, that it may impart grace to the hearers" (Eph. 4:29, NKJV). Jezebel's threats qualify as corrupt communication, but the eunuchs are deceived and see those receiving their demonic messages as the true threat to the kingdom.

We know that the "words of a talebearer are as wounds, and they go down into the innermost parts of the body" (Prov. 18:8). That's what Jezebel wants—for its negative words to go down into the innermost parts of your soul and unleash demonic imaginations against your mind that influence your behavior. King David admonished us to keep our tongues from evil and our lips from speaking deceit (Ps. 34:13). Jezebel doesn't care about the fate of the eunuchs, who will have to give can account to Jesus for every idle word they speak (Matt. 12:36) and will be condemned rather than justified for those words (Matt. 12:37) if they don't repent. We'll talk more about how eunuchs can break free from Jezebel's grip in the next chapter. For now let's look at what causes them to stand by Jezebel until a Jehu arrives to deliver them.

Eunuchs Seek Jezebel's Praise

As I mentioned in chapter 2, eunuchs were expected to do the bidding of their masters. Since society held eunuchs in low esteem—eunuchs, for example, were not allowed to serve as part of the Levitical priesthood because of their "defect"—they could be removed or even killed for disobedience without much thought. Eunuchs, then, were usually faithful to perform their duties—though not always truly loyal to their masters.

As we learned in the section above, Queen Jezebel took advantage of her high position in society—and the eunuch's low position—to handle tasks that helped her advance her evil plots. Like today's spiritual eunuchs, some likely performed out of religious duty and others likely performed because they loved the praise of the leadership. Fear, hurts, wounds, and all the insecurities that go along with those fears and wounds also played a role.

In the modern-day church eunuchs aren't physically castrated. They are spiritually castrated. In other words, they may appear to have some spiritual authority in a church setting, but in reality they've been stripped of their spiritual strength to resist the wiles of Jezebelic personalities because they are deceived. I should mention that modern-day spiritual eunuchs don't always serve the leadership. Sometimes they are controlled by Jezebelic church members working to erect their own power structure within the church.

Whether they succumb to a religious mind-set or the pursuit of the praise of man, eunuchs are powerless to rise up against Jezebel in their own strength. They are effectively in bondage to a strongman they didn't see binding them. Without any true power or authority of their own, eunuchs live vicariously through Jezebel and draw their strength from the approval of Jezebel—or more specifically those flowing in a Jezebel spirit—rather than the approval of God. This is a dangerous position to take and is called out in Scripture.

Paul understood how vital it was to keep his heart in line with what God wanted rather than what man wanted. Paul made it known in no uncertain terms that he was seeking the approval of God and not man (Gal. 1:10), and the Bible is clear that the fear of man lays a snare but whoever trusts in the Lord is safe (Prov. 29:25). Ultimately eunuchs "fear those who kill the body" but can't kill the soul rather than fearing "Him who is able to destroy both soul and body in hell" (Matt. 10:28). Spiritual eunuchs today do this because they are deceived.

We'll talk about how that deception overtook them in a moment. First, let's look at how Jezebel leverages the spirit of religion to castrate believers and make them eunuchs. The spirit of religion—a murderous spirit of legalism that influenced the Pharisees—works with the spirit of Jezebel to lay a trap. John the Apostle exposed this when he wrote: "Yet many of the rulers also believed in Him. But because of the Pharisees they did not confess Him, lest they be put out of the synagogue. For they loved the praise of men more than the praise of God" (John 12:42–43).

Indeed, the Bible has plenty to say about seeking to please man versus seeking to please God, and it's the former that allows Jezebel to entrap its eunuchs. Paul told the Thessalonians that he spoke "not to please men, but God, who examines our hearts" (1 Thess. 2:4). You can't serve two masters. You can't serve your desire for power and God at the same time any more than you can serve your desire for money and God at the same time. You can't serve the flesh and the Spirit at the same time:

> For the flesh lusts against the Spirit, and the Spirit against the flesh. These are in opposition to one another, so that you may not do the things that

> you please. But if you are led by the Spirit, you are not under the law.
>
> —GALATIANS 5:17–18

And if you are led by the Spirit, you are not under legalism. If you are led by the Spirit, you are not under Jezebel. The question is why do eunuchs fall into this snare of seeking to please man (or the one flowing in a Jezebel spirit) rather than God? The answer is hidden insecurities, rejection, and fears. But I believe the root of the issue is the spirit of rejection.

WHY EUNUCHS SUBMIT TO JEZEBEL

Remember Mindy? She battled rejection since she was old enough to understand that her father left on the day she was born. A spirit of rejection crept into her soul that plagued her life from that day forward. She always felt as if she had to earn the approval of her mother and her brothers and her sisters. She felt as if she had to earn the approval of men, who took advantage of her sexually. And when she got saved, she felt as if she had to earn the approval of the pastor. Ultimately she sometimes unknowingly sought the approval of Jezebel.

In my book *The Heart of the Prophetic* I outline several of Jezebel's playgrounds, including insecurities, hidden fears, and rejection. Think about it for a minute. Eunuchs in Bible days were largely rejected by mainstream society. They were essentially well-treated slaves in kings' palaces, always seeing the best of everything but never experiencing any of it. Isaiah talked about how God's people could be made eunuchs of enemies:

> Then Isaiah said to Hezekiah, "Hear the word of the LORD of Hosts. The days are surely coming when all that is in your house, and that which your fathers have laid up in store until this day, shall be carried to Babylon. Nothing shall be left, says the LORD. And some of your sons who descend from you, whom you shall father, shall be taken away. And they shall become officials in the palace of the king of Babylon."
>
> —ISAIAH 39:5–7

This happened after Hezekiah decided to align himself with Babylon. When Christians decide to align themselves with the ungodly, then captivity—and ultimately slavery, condemnation, and feelings of worthlessness and rejection—can result from this sin. Babylon was the mother of idolatry and part of Jezebel's religious system. Babylon is essentially the world's religion that spews forth doctrines of demons. The Book of Revelation reveals Babylon as both a religious system and an economic system that seduces people in the last days. (See Revelation 14:8; 17:1–6; 18:2–10.)

I dive deeper into the connection between Jezebel and Babylon in my book *The Spiritual Warrior's Guide to Defeating Jezebel*, so I won't get into all the theology here. I just wanted to show you that God's people can be taken captive and made into eunuchs. Of course, in today's church we're talking about spiritual eunuchs. Again, I believe people fall into this trap because they seek the praise of men over the praise of God—and their actions often are rooted in insecurities, hidden fears, and rejection.

I wrote this in my book *The Heart of the Prophetic*:

> Because everybody is insecure about something, no one is immune to Jezebel. Jezebel probes your soul to discover your insecurities and hidden fears so that she can exploit them later. Flattery works well on folks who have insecurities and hidden fears or rejection. Jezebel can smooth talk them. Jezebel can tell them how great a singer they are or how powerful a preacher they are. Whether it's true or not, they'll receive it because they want to. It makes them feel better about their insecure selves. Then Jezebel can manipulate and tap into their pride. Jezebel will tell them how they should be elevated to a more visible position in the ministry. Jezebel will tell them how their gift should be making room for them.[3]

I'll share more about that in a moment. Suffice it to say that Jezebel will seek to control you by petting your insecurities and alleviating your hidden fears. What are you insecure about? What are you afraid of? Our confidence should be in Christ in us—and He hasn't given us a spirit of fear, but of power, love, and a sound mind (2 Tim. 1:7). It may seem like a pedestrian scripture, but if we really had a revelation of it then I believe the body of Christ would rise up and take dominion rather than lying down in timidity and watching sinners eat the good of the land. Prophets need to get this so they can herald it, but as long as prophets are bound up with rejection, Jezebel will get the best of them.

One of my prophetic mentors has said, "You can't have a prophet full of rejection." Why is that? Because it opens the door for Jezebel. Jezebel targets hurts and wounds, and unfortunately many prophets—and many people in general—have a root of rejection. It may be that you were different, even from your childhood years. It may be that the local church doesn't understand your gift and has rejected you along with God's voice. Rejection comes through many channels, and it's poison for the prophet because it opens the door to control, fear of man, fear of failure, and a host of other ungodly emotions.

We must get free from rejection—continually examining our hearts for traces of this disease—so we don't find ourselves eating at Jezebel's dinner table with the company of false prophets or serving in Jezebel's bedchambers. We'll talk more about how to break free from the eunuch spirit in the next chapter. For now, let's talk about how to discern—and deal with—Jezebel's eunuchs in our midst.

Discerning Jezebel's Eunuchs

If you've heard me say it once, you've heard me say it a number of times—we can't go on witch hunts for spirits. Or at least we shouldn't. That's not how the Holy Spirit works, and it can lead us into false accusations against God's people—or worse, it can lead us into deception that blinds us to what's truly operating because we've proudly concluded by our own wisdom that this, that, or the other spirit is operating. I don't know about you, but I don't want to sow those kinds of seeds in my field. If the Holy Spirit isn't showing me, I don't want to see it.

Whether it's Jezebel, witchcraft, religion, Ahab, or eunuchs, we need to be careful not to apply information and revelation in a reckless manner about how spirits operate. A "reckless manner" would be using information and revelation to label people in your church, workplace, or home as Jezebels, Ahabs, eunuchs, false prophets—or anything else. It's harmful to the person you are falsely accusing, but it's also harmful to your own soul. What's more, it does not please God. Again, I don't want to sow those kinds of seeds in my field. If the Holy Spirit isn't showing me, I don't want to see it.

I speak from experience. I once attended a church where this practice was commonplace. When people walked in the door, they often were pegged before the end of the first service. Typically they supposedly had either a religious or Jezebel spirit, or they were full of rejection and fear, or they were just downright rebellious. Most of the time this wasn't discernment operating. It was the insecurities and fears of those engaging in the witch hunt. These witch hunters were usually leaders serving the Jezebelic pastor, and they didn't want anyone else taking their place. So if they didn't feel as if they could control a newcomer—if they felt threatened—that newcomer was falsely demonized and quickly ostracized.

Of course, everyone wasn't automatically labeled when they came through the door. Some were celebrated and given positions of service in the church—until they did something leadership didn't like, such as put family before ministry, fail to give enough to the latest fund-raiser, or otherwise not conform to the leadership's overbearing demands. At that point it was common for the person to be labeled a Jezebel. Seeds of discord then were sown in the congregation against that person so others would start to back off from them until the "Jezebel" finally felt so rejected the person left the church. Essentially anyone who was friendly with a person the leaders labeled a Jezebel was called out as a eunuch and shunned.

How do you recognize a modern-day eunuch? Eunuchs help forward Jezebel's agenda, knowingly or unknowingly. Sometimes people mistake those flowing as eunuchs with those flowing in a Jezebel spirit. You need the Holy Spirit to show you the difference, but the bottom line is that eunuchs don't hatch the controlling, seducing plans. Eunuchs merely help Jezebel execute her wishes.

Dealing With Jezebel's Eunuchs

As I mentioned, I attended a church that was super focused on the spirit of Jezebel, and eventually Ahab and eunuchs, and anyone who was friendly with a person the leadership labeled a Jezebel was called out as a eunuch and shunned. This is a sad approach. If someone really is flowing in a Jezebel spirit and has "spiritual children" and "students" who are spying for them, godly spiritual leadership would seek to deliver them from this spirit's clutches rather than trying to chase them out of the church.

If you discern one of Jezebel's eunuchs in your midst—someone who seems to be on assignment for a person flowing in this wicked spirit—take caution. Remember, eunuchs are Jezebel's servants and have a somewhat intimate relationship with her. Whatever their motivation or however they got trapped in Jezebel's witchcraft, eunuchs may be deceived or may be looking for a way of escape.

Take the situation to God in prayer and seek wisdom from the Holy Spirit. You could be the Jehu that gives them the boldness to throw Jezebel down. In other words, by reaching out with bold truth in love to one who is serving the Jezebel spirit's purposes, you could help them break free from this evil influence. But you could also fall into Jezebel's trap and wind up in a spiritual battle you aren't called to enter. Again, pray, seek wise counsel, and follow the Holy Spirit. The same Holy Spirit who reveals the eunuchs to you will instruct you how to move forward in the situation.

In the next chapter we'll take a deeper look at how to escape this spiritual slavery.

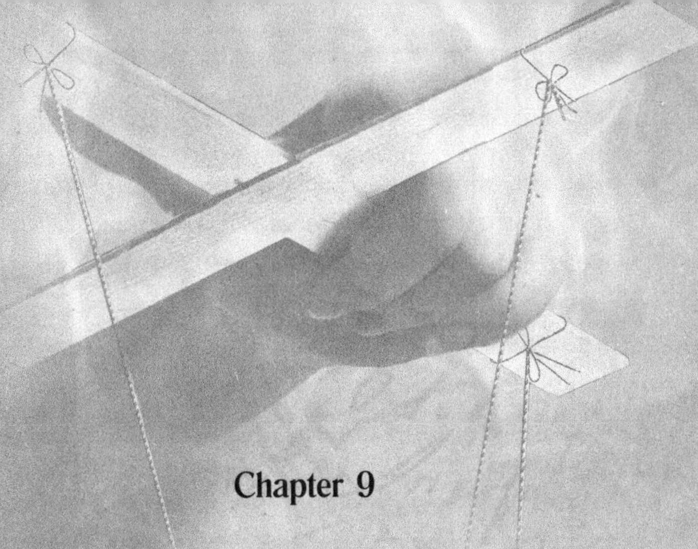

Chapter 9

ESCAPING SPIRITUAL SLAVERY

MINDY WAS A spiritual slave—but she thought she was a spiritual master. Mindy was in Pastor Jake's inner circle, but she never discerned that Jezebel was drawing lines, Ahab was pressing her buttons, and false prophets were propping her up while she and other spiritual eunuchs executed his wicked will.

In her enthusiasm to serve God and in her lack of experience with spiritual warfare, Mindy failed to take the Apostle Paul's advice on Christian liberty: "Stand fast therefore in the liberty by which Christ has made us free, and do not be entangled again with a yoke of bondage" (Gal. 5:1, NKJV).

Of course, Paul was talking about believers who were still trying to find justification by the Law, but he also asked: "O foolish Galatians! Who has bewitched you that you should not obey the truth? Before your eyes Jesus

Christ was clearly portrayed among you as crucified" (Gal. 3:1). The word *bewitched* in that verse is telling. It comes from the Greek word *baskaino*, which means "to charm, to bewitch."[1]

And this is just what Jezebel does to woo its eunuchs. Although Queen Jezebel's eunuchs served by force, the Jezebel spirit's eunuchs are manipulated into service. Jezebel seeks out those who, like natural eunuchs who have been castrated, lack an understanding of their identity in Christ, or are suffering from low self-esteem or hurts and wounds. Jezebel builds them up with flattering words of appreciation until it entangles them again with its yoke of bondage. As we discussed earlier in the book, this is exactly what happened to Mindy. But there is hope for Mindy and those like her.

Indeed, Jezebel's spiritual eunuchs may be at its beck and call, but they are hardly loyal. Once these eunuchs understand how controlling, manipulative, and otherwise evil Jezebel is, they seek a way of escape. Unfortunately it's not always so easy to break off relationship with Jezebel. First, this spirit won't let you go without a fight. Second, there are often soul ties between the person operating in a Jezebel spirit and their eunuchs because these spiritual slaves grow dependent on its leading (instead of the leading of the Holy Spirit). In this chapter you'll discover how to pray for the deliverance of eunuchs or how to break free yourself.

Jezebel's Spiritual Abuse

It's been said the anointing comes at a cost—and so does working in Jezebel's bedchambers. It may seem like a privilege to work in the bedchambers of spiritual leaders, but one can only imagine the level of spiritual abuse at the hands of leadership that is operating in Jezebel and Ahab spirits. Spiritual abuse plays at both ends of the eunuch equation. Jezebel makes eunuchs out of wounded soldiers by spiritually abusing them when they accept false praise. But after eunuchs enter into Jezebel's bedchambers, the spiritual abuse escalates.

What exactly is spiritual abuse? Jeff VanVonderen, coauthor of the classic book *The Subtle Power of Spiritual Abuse*, explains it this way: "Spiritual abuse occurs when someone in a position of spiritual authority...misuses that authority, placing themselves over God's people to control, coerce or manipulate them for seemingly godly purposes which are really their own."[2]

When spiritual leaders are caught in sex-abuse scandals, the secular and Christian media alike pen stories that offer the detestable details and dogged denials. But spiritual abuse, cultish churches, and controlling ministries are less often exposed than pastors who coerce teenage boys and unsuspecting church secretaries to have sexual relations.

Victims of abusive church authority structures may not even realize what they are enduring until they escape its grip. Spiritual abuse is often subtle. Christian cult leaders don't always operate like Peoples Temple leader Jim Jones, who led a mass murder-suicide of his members in 1978. Controlling ministries tend to hide behind the guise of spiritual coverings. And far too many outsiders are not willing even to question the messages and practices of such churches. It takes lovers of truth with spiritual discernment to recognize the sometimes subtle signs of abusive churches. And it takes courage to confront the abuse.

Spiritual abuse is hardly a new phenomenon. You can find instances in the Bible of spiritual leaders exploiting people to build their kingdoms. In Jeremiah 8 the Lord called out the abuse of prophets and priests, saying, "They dress the wound of my people as though it were not serious" (v. 11, NIV).

The root problems of people in the "church" were treated superficially. In other words, the pastor put a Band-Aid on the problem so things looked good from the outside, but the wound was festering on the inside. The pastor's prominence was more important than the legitimate needs of the congregation.

Today this manifests as spiritual leaders recruiting volunteers to build their ministries while neglecting to minister to the real needs of hurting people. In such cases, churches become like businesses. The pastor is more like a CEO than a spiritual leader. Staff meetings center on marketing initiatives that will bring more people—who will bring more tithes and offerings—into the sanctuary. Church services become about external appearances, but the white-washed tombs are full of dead men's bones.

Jesus addressed spiritual abuse in His day. Beyond His warnings about the Pharisees, Jesus also pointed out "ravenous wolves" (Matt. 7:15). These ravenous wolves look much like anointed prophets, but their motives are dastardly. Today the spiritually abusive pharisaical pastor has a long list of rules and demands and little grace for those who don't rise to the occasion.

RECOGNIZING SPIRITUAL ABUSE

Entire books have been written on spiritual abuse. Those books will help you see spiritual abuse for what it is, how you got sucked into the cycle, how to break free from spiritual abuse, and how to recover from spiritual abuse once you've escaped its clutches. But for now I want to offer you some nuggets from Dave Johnson and VanVonderen's book, *The Subtle Power of Spiritual Abuse.*

Power-posturing is a telltale sign of spiritual abuse.

"Power-posturing leaders spend a lot of time focused on their own authority and reminding others of it," write Johnson and VanVonderen. The authors say this is necessary because those leaders' spiritual authority isn't real—based on genuine godly character—it is postured.[3]

From my experience, this might manifest as a leader who likes to remind the congregation that he can excommunicate people or that any anointing you are flowing in comes from the head (him). This leader can never be questioned and is usually not accountable to anyone. Those around him are usually mere yes-men who do his bidding in exchange for delegated authority to lord over others.

Performance preoccupation is a sign of spiritual abuse.

Johnson and VanVonderen note that *obedience* and *submission* are two important words often used in abusive church structures. Don't get me wrong. Obedience and submission are important. But spiritual abuse often shames or scares people into obedience and submission. True obedience is a matter of the heart. Spiritual abusers apply undue pressure that is not from God. That pressure is usually applied to get you to do the leader's will, not God's will.

Unspoken rules are common in instances of spiritual abuse. In abusive spiritual systems, Johnson and VanVonderen offer, people's lives are controlled from the outside in by rules, spoken and unspoken: "Unspoken rules are those that govern unhealthy churches or families but are not said out loud. Because they are not said out loud, you don't find out that they're there until you break them," they write. It often seems these "rules" hold more power than Scripture.[4]

The "can't talk" rule is seen where spiritual abuse is present.

Johnson and VanVonderen explain that the "can't talk" rule blames the person who talks, and the ensuing punishments pressure questioners into silence.[5]

I'll never forget the day I realized that if you voice a problem you become the problem. If you question why the church no longer picks up the poor kids in the ministry van but has shifted its focus to more affluent neighborhoods, you are removed from your role as a volunteer driver. Others see your fate and decide they'd better not rock the boat. It's a form of intimidation.

Lack of balance and extremism is often present where spiritual abuse lives. This manifests as an unbalanced approach to living out the truth of the Christian life. Johnson and VanVonderen explain that in these systems it is more important to act according to the word of a leader who has "a word" for you than to act according to what you know to be true from Scripture, or simply from your spiritual-growth history.

The truth is, prophetic words don't carry the same weight as Scripture, and you can hear from God for yourself. When you rely on other people to tell you what God is saying, you open the door to control and manipulation.

It's not possible to fully expose the inner workings of spiritual abuse, Christian cults, and controlling churches in a single chapter. My goal is to raise awareness of a troubling issue and get you thinking—not to send you on a witch hunt for spiritual abusers.

If you think you are part of a spiritually abusive, cultlike, or controlling church, ask the Lord to break any deception off your mind and show you the truth. The truth could be that you are in a healthy church and you just need to die to self. But it could be that you are in an abusive system and you need to break free. If your heart is purely seeking the truth, the Holy Spirit will surely guide you there (John 16:13).

Breaking Free From Jezebel's Lordship

Remember Jezebel's strategy for recruiting eunuchs: this opportunistic spirit targets people who are emotionally or spiritually damaged. To break free from Jezebel's lordship in your life you need to break free from the hurts and wounds that gave Jezebel entry. Until you are fully healed, you won't be fully able to resist Jezebel's manipulative flattery because you will crave to hear kind words even if you know unkind actions follow. It's a classic pattern of abuse.

On the flip side of this demonic coin, Jezebel will

wound you so it can control you. This is why it's so vital not to stuff your pain deep into your soul, thinking you'll deal with it later. If someone hurts you, deal with it now. Don't wait. Go to the Lord immediately in prayer and ask Him to soothe your emotions, heal your heart, and strengthen your spirit man.

Listen, when you are wounded, the hurt you feel is real, and pretending as if you aren't hurt isn't going to bring healing any more than pretending your leg isn't broken is going to make it possible to walk rightly. Sometimes when we get hurt in church, folks like to tell us we have no reason to feel bad and that we just need to get over it. Half that statement is true. We do need to get over it, but it's not always true that we have no reason to feel bad. If someone close to you is spewing malicious gossip behind your back and you find out about it, it can sting.

No matter what kind of hurt you're dealing with, don't rush into a confrontation with the offender. Again, take it to God in prayer. Psalm 50:15 says, "Call on Me in the day of trouble." That works for a troubled soul just as well as it does any other trouble. Tell Him how you feel and ask Him to heal your wounds. It may be that the Lord is going to deal with the offender directly and anything you say would just make matters worse. Of course, it could be that the Lord will give you a graceful way to explain why you feel hurt. If you take it to God, He can give you the very words to say to your offender (Luke 12:12). And He can bring conviction to that person's heart when you approach him with a spirit of humility (John 16:8).

Whatever you do, don't retaliate. In His Sermon on

the Mount Jesus teaches us to turn the other cheek (Matt. 5:39) and to love our enemies, bless those who curse us, do good to those who hate us, and pray for those who spitefully use us and persecute us (v. 44).

With that in mind, don't go around telling everybody what someone did to hurt your feelings. Think about it for a minute. That makes it all too easy for Jezebel. When someone operates in a Jezebel spirit, they actively seek those who are hurt and wounded in an information-seeking mission that aims to ensnare another victim. Going around telling everyone how hurt you are is like inviting a visit from Jezebel. Keep your pain between you and the Lord or between you and a close confidant you know can tightly shut their lips.

And don't make accusations against those who hurt you if you decide to confront the matter. You don't want to move in the same spirit they are moving in—or in the flesh. Instead of saying, "You hurt my feelings!" say, "When you did that I felt hurt," or, "When you talk to me like that I feel upset." Own your feelings because they are your feelings. It's very possible that your offender has no idea that what they said or did hurt you—and never meant to hurt you. If you approach the person in humility, seeking reconciliation, your offender may be quick to apologize. You will then slam the door shut on the enemy—whether it's Jezebel, bitterness, or anything else.

You Can't Heal Until You Forgive

Peter exhorts us to "above all things, have unfailing love for one another, because love covers a multitude of sins" (1 Pet. 4:8). Again, be led by the Holy Spirit. It's not always necessary to go to someone who hurt you every time the person does something you don't like.

It could be that the Lord is working something out that's in you. Maybe you're too sensitive. Maybe you are easy prey for spirits like Jezebel because you are quick to anger and offense and slow to forgive and forget. We always need to check our hearts. Is the person really being hurtful, or are we looking at it through filters of past hurts or rejection or anger that cloud the truth? Ask the Lord. Or it could be that the Holy Spirit will bring conviction—maybe even heap coals of fire on his head—as you bless him outwardly with a heart of love. This hurt issue is serious business. Bitterness can kill you.

The bottom line is this: it doesn't matter how wrong your offender is, you have to forgive. Forgiveness is not for the other person—it's for you. Forgiveness doesn't justify what someone did that was wrong, nor does it necessarily mean that the relationship goes right back to where it was. Sometimes trust needs to be reestablished. Sometimes reconciliation is just not possible. Nevertheless, if you don't forgive, you end up bitter and resentful, and before too long you'll end up hurting other people. The healing process can't really begin until you spit out the bait of offense. I'll leave you with this prophetic insight the Holy Spirit gave me once when I was extremely hurt in church:

> When the feeling of hurt arises, the spirit of offense comes on the scene to fortify the pain, tempting you to hold on to the grudge in your

heart. Therefore, the proper response to emotional pain of the soul is always an immediate confession of forgiveness from the heart. The alternative to forgiveness from the heart is the ongoing torment of the soul. So if you want to be free from your hurts and wounds, take thoughts of forgiveness, meditate on them, and confess them rather than taking thoughts of the hurt, meditating on them, and confessing them. This is God's way—and it's the only way that brings true healing. And, while you are at it, pray for those who have hurt you. This process will cleanse your heart and renew your mind. And you will walk free from the pain of your past.

Amen.

Mirror, Mirror on the Wall!

In order to break free from Jezebel's spiritual abuse, you need to look in a new mirror. Jezebel wants you to look in its mirror. Like the evil queen in the fairy tale *Snow White*, that mirror will tell you that Jezebel is the fairest of them all after this spirit strips you of your identity in Christ.

You remember the story: The evil queen had a magic mirror. Every morning she approached the mirror and asked: "Mirror, mirror on the wall, who's the fairest of them all?" One day the mirror replied: "My Queen, you are the fairest here, so true. But Snow White is a thousand times more beautiful than you." The evil queen was enraged and hired a huntsman to murder Snow White and deliver her lungs and liver. The huntsman did not obey the evil queen's command, and her plot to poison Snow White with an apple also failed.

Ultimately the evil queen died, and Snow White lived happily ever after with her prince. That isn't exactly a prophetic picture of Jezebel, but there are parallels—especially for eunuchs who escape Jezebel's puppet show and marry Jesus, the Prince of Peace, and get a full revelation of who they are in Him by looking into His supernatural mirror of love. This mirror gives you assurance that you are the most cherished of them all. This mirror transforms us from glory to glory. It's called the Bible, the Word of God, the Holy Scripture. And its authors, inspired by the Holy Spirit, compared it to a mirror on three occasions. By exploring the Bible as a mirror, we gain a clearer understanding of how to become more like the holiest of all.

Do you speak in tongues? So did Paul the apostle. But he would be the first to tell you that without love it meant little more than sounding brass and clanging cymbals (1 Cor. 13:1). Can you prophesy an accurate word in due season? Paul could prophesy with the best of them, and he understood the mystery of Christ. Do you move in the gift of faith? Paul did. Yet without love, Paul confessed, he would have been nothing. Do you give to the poor? Would you be willing to die for the cause of Christ? That's awesome. But if you aren't motivated by love, it won't do you a bit of good in eternity.

The truth is, prophecies will fail, tongues will cease, and knowledge will vanish away. We know in part and we prophesy in part. We won't be perfect until we trade this mortality for immortality, this corruption for incorruption. But we must steadily mature along the narrow path, even if we can't see clearly where we are going. We walk by faith and not by sight. And we have to focus on what matters. What matters most are faith, hope, and love. Paul put it this way:

> When I was a child, I spoke as a child, I understood as a child, and I thought as a child. But when I became a man, I put away childish things. For now we see as through a glass, dimly, but then, face to face. Now I know in part, but then I shall know, even as I also am known. So now abide faith, hope, and love, these three. But the greatest of these is love.
>
> —1 CORINTHIANS 13:11–13

LOOKING INTO GOD'S MIRROR

When we look into the Word of God, the true mirror, it builds faith, restores hope, and inspires love in our hearts for God, ourselves, and others. When we turn to the Lord—and when we turn through the pages of His Word seeking His truth—the veil is taken away. In other words, our minds are renewed. And we are transformed by the renewing of our minds as the Spirit of God supernaturally reveals the Word of God with such clear understanding that we are never the same:

> Now the Lord is the Spirit. And where the Spirit of the Lord is, there is liberty. But we all, seeing the glory of the Lord with unveiled faces, as in a

> mirror, are being transformed into the same image from glory to glory by the Spirit of the Lord.
>
> —2 CORINTHIANS 3:17–18

Now here's the rub. As we look into the mirror that is the Word of God, we must believe what it says about who we are, and we must do what it says we should do by the grace of God. Otherwise, we walk away with a spirit of deception hot on our trail. James said it better than I can:

> Be doers of the word and not hearers only, deceiving yourselves. For if anyone is a hearer of the word and not a doer, he is like a man viewing his natural face in a mirror. He views himself, and goes his way, and immediately forgets what kind of man he was.
>
> —JAMES 1:22–24

The mirror tells us who we are. We are holy as He is holy. We are the righteousness of God in Christ Jesus. Greater is He who is in us than he that is in the world. We are the head and not the tail, above and not beneath. We are more than conquerors in Christ. I could go on and on about who you are in Christ. The mirror speaks clearly. And there's an interesting correlation here between our behavior and the revelation of who we are.

I believe that when we fail to walk in the revealed light of God's Word to us, it robs us of the confidence of who we are in Him. Sin—failing to do the Word—causes a breach in our fellowship with God. It brings guilt, shame, and condemnation. When we sin, we have to remember who we are in Christ—the forgiven—and quickly repent.

Then we need to go back and look in the mirror again to find out who we are. The more time we spend in front of the mirror looking at who we are, the less often we'll stumble. A revelation of who we are is a mighty weapon against the enemy. When we put that revelation into words, it becomes a spiritual sword. Look out, devil!

Our ultimate goal is to be transformed into the image of Christ. The writer of Hebrews offers us hope:

> Going through a long line of prophets, God has been addressing our ancestors in different ways for centuries. Recently he spoke to us directly through his Son. By his Son, God created the world in the beginning, and it will all belong to the Son at the end. This Son perfectly mirrors God, and is stamped with God's nature. He holds everything together by what he says—powerful words!
>
> —Hebrews 1:1–3, the message

The Son perfectly mirrors God. One day we will perfectly mirror the Son. Until then let us look into the mirror of God's Word to seek the face of the holiest One of all—and let us speak forth the revelation of who we are in Christ—and who we will be in eternity. And remember this: Jesus is your Jehu. In other words, you don't need a person to come along and set you free from Jezebel's bedchambers. If you have been serving as Jezebel's eunuch, Jesus will set you free. You have to first acknowledge that you've committed sin by allowing Jezebel to use you.

Delivering the Eunuchs

If you know someone who has fallen into Jezebel's trap and is serving faithfully as a eunuch, it's not always easy to set them free, but it is possible. No matter how knowledgeable you are about spiritual warfare and deliverance, you cannot come to a eunuch (or any other spiritual captive) with persuasive words of human wisdom. You must approach the situation with a demonstration of the Spirit and of power (1 Cor. 2:4).

First, you need to be led by the Holy Spirit to approach the eunuch, or you won't stand much chance of being heard. Until you get a witness from the Holy Spirit to approach the eunuch, your job is to pray that God would break in with light and allow the eunuch to see Jezebel for what it really is. Your assignment is to intercede for the eunuch's awakening and deliverance from a distance. The Holy Spirit will lead you to approach the eunuch at the right time and give you words of wisdom to speak to their soul that will fully remove the blinders from their eyes. The eunuch must want to break free and repent for allowing the enemy to put them in bondage before deliverance can take place.

Once the eunuch sees that Jezebel has spiritually enslaved him, renounces the spirit, and repents with godly sorrow to the Lord, you can set out on a course of deliverance. However, your first action is not to discern a devil to cast out. Your first action is to provide information and help the eunuch seek further revelation of what is working behind the spiritual scenes. You must co-labor with Christ to help the eunuch understand how he was enslaved so he can work with the Holy Spirit to shore up the areas of his soul that allowed Jezebel entrance.

The person operating in the Jezebel spirit may try to discredit you when the Holy Spirit sends you on a rescue mission to restore the eunuch. Prepare yourself for the attack, which typically comes in the form of false accusations or spiritual witchcraft. Prepare the eunuch for the attack against you, letting the person know that this is a typical tactic Jezebel uses to keep eunuchs in bondage.

Also, prepare yourself and the eunuch for the retaliation that will come when Jesus sets the captive free. In other words, Jezebel still won't give up the fight for a soul to control. Be ready to resist witchcraft. When you cast out devils by the finger of God, then the kingdom of God has come to you (Luke 11:20). But what comes next isn't always as much fun. There is often natural and spiritual retaliation for setting the captives free.

Although no weapon formed against a deliverance minister can prosper, the enemy nonetheless forms a weapon and takes his best shot. After all, when you cast out devils—when you set the captives free—you do marked damage to the kingdom of darkness. Whether you are an experienced deliverance minister or just beginning to study the gospel art of casting out devils, entering the battle without expecting the backlash is not wise.

Readying for Jezebel's Retaliation

I've cast devils out of people only to turn around and face a heavy dose of witchcraft or imaginations that tried to convince me the devil never left. I've had nightmares after exercising deliverance ministry. I've felt tired and sick. Thankfully I understood that it was the enemy hitting back and took authority over the assignment in the name of Jesus.

When you set out to engage in deliverance ministry, don't go there without preparing your heart—and don't go there alone. Jesus sent the seventy disciples out two by two to cast out devils (Luke 10:1). And they understood their authority in the name of Jesus before they ventured into ministry. Deliverance ministry is not a game of patty-cake.

To be sure, you can't just read *Pigs in the Parlor* and dub yourself a deliverance minister. If you don't truly understand your authority in Christ—if you don't have an intimate relationship with Him—the retaliation could be dramatic and painful. Remember the itinerant Jewish exorcists who took it upon themselves to call the name of the Lord Jesus over those who had evil spirits?

They said, "We exorcise you by the Jesus whom Paul preaches." The seven sons of Sceva joined into the deliverance party, and "the evil spirit answered, 'I know Jesus, and I know Paul, but who are you?' Then the man in whom the evil spirit was jumped on them, overpowered them, and prevailed against them, so that they fled from that house naked and wounded" (Acts 19:15–16).

Although you aren't likely to experience anything quite like what happened to the sons of Sceva, that doesn't mean you shouldn't prepare yourself for retaliation before you ever step foot into a deliverance session. Beyond fasting, seeking God for wisdom, and putting together a team of deliverance ministers, remember to bind up the retaliation and plead the blood of Jesus over yourself before and after the session. And everything you do, do with faith in the name of Jesus.

In terms of deliverance itself for the eunuch, there are entire books written on the topic of deliverance. *Pigs in the Parlor* is a classic, but it's also a good idea to work alongside experienced deliverance ministers before trying to tackle deliverance on your own. The bottom line is, we have authority over demons and we can cast them out in the name of Jesus, just as Jesus did when He walked the earth.

Although you may find success in casting devils out of a person who has not gone through a process of renouncing, repenting, and forgiving, it's dangerous ground to cast out a devil and leave an open door for its return. Jesus once said:

> When an unclean spirit goes out of a man, it passes through dry places seeking rest, but finds none. Then it says, "I will return to my house from which I came." And when it comes, it finds it empty, swept, and put in order. Then it goes and brings with itself seven other spirits more evil than itself, and they enter and dwell there. And the last state of that man is worse than the first. So shall it be also with this evil generation.
>
> —Matthew 12:43–45

Throw Jezebel Down

After someone has forgiven those who hurt them, received God's healing for hurts and wounds, and embraced who they really are in Christ, Jezebel often will flee when confronted in the spirit in the name of Jesus. Once we've effectively submitted ourselves to God and resisted the devil, he must flee (James 4:7). But that doesn't mean he'll flee for good. That's why the goal is to seal up the doorways of entrance.

Again, this bears repeating: to slam the door completely shut on Jezebel and its puppets, you (or the person you are ministering to) may need to break soul ties with Jezebel, renounce the relationship, and ask the Lord to forgive you for aligning yourself with that spirit. If you need a reminder about breaking soul ties, go back to chapter 8.

Jesus doesn't want you merely to walk away from Jezebel. He wants you to throw this spirit down. In other words, Jesus wants you to cast out any trace of Jezebel from your life. Jesus wants you to take authority over the spirit that had authority over you. Jesus wants you to do this not only for yourself, but also for others who may also be enslaved in Jezebel's bedchambers. Jezebel will not go down without a fight, but if you stand strong against this spirit—or people operating in this spirit—you will throw it down in your life for good.

Jezebel wants to use eunuchs as her puppets, but God has a bigger purpose to use them to deliver His people from this spirit. Remember, Jesus is your Jehu. Jesus has already conquered Jezebel and any other spiritual enemy that rises up against you to defy His will for your life. The Spirit that raised Christ from the dead dwells in you! (See Romans 8:11.) If God is for you, who can be against you? (See Romans 8:31.) Even if you have become one of

Jezebel's eunuchs, freedom is a decision away. Let me leave you with this account to remind you of the importance eunuchs play in delivering God's people from the evil influence of Jezebel:

> When Jehu came to Jezreel, Jezebel heard about it. She put black paint on her eyes, adorned her head, and looked down through the window. As Jehu entered in at the gate, she said, "Is everything all right, Zimri, murderer of his master?"
>
> And he lifted up his face toward the window and said, "Who is on my side? Who?" And two or three eunuchs looked down to him. He said, "Drop her down." So they dropped her down and some of her blood splattered on the wall and on the horses. Then he trampled her. Then he entered, ate and drank, and said, "Attend to that cursed woman and bury her, for she is a king's daughter." So they went to bury her, but they found nothing of her except a skull, the feet, and the palms of her hands. They returned and told Jehu, and he said, "This is the word of the LORD, which He spoke by His servant Elijah the Tishbite, saying, 'On the property of Jezreel dogs will eat the flesh of Jezebel. The corpse of Jezebel will be like dung in the field on the property of Jezreel, so that they cannot say, This is Jezebel.'"
>
> —2 KINGS 9:30–37

Whether you have discovered you are operating as a eunuch, know someone struggling to break free from Jezebel's bedchambers, or are preparing to help a eunuch reclaim his rightful identity in Christ, let those verses encourage your heart. God used Jehu to strengthen the eunuchs, but these spiritual captives are the ones who rose up in the strength of God and threw her down. Not only that, but also these eunuchs buried the witch and were instruments to fulfill a prophecy that changed a nation.

In the next chapter we'll take a look at a different enemy: Jezebel's children.

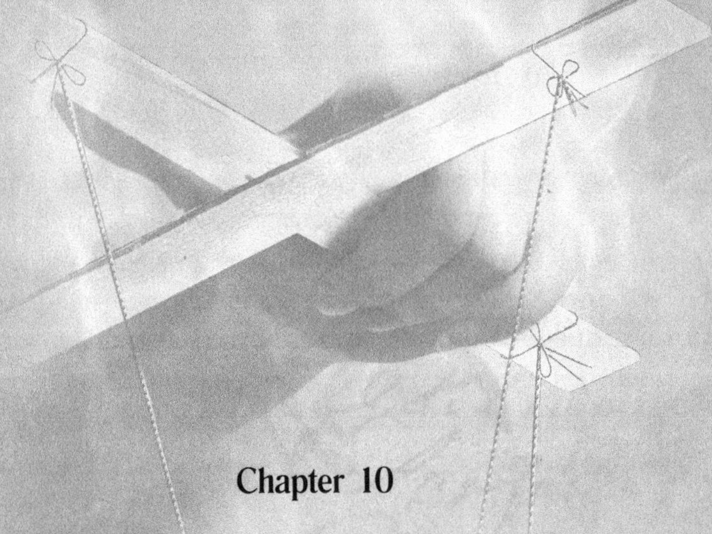

Chapter 10

RECOGNIZING JEZEBEL'S SPIRITUAL CHILDREN

YOU'VE HEARD IT said, "Like mother, like daughter," and, "Like father, like son." Such clichés are troublingly true in the Jezebel-Ahab family dynamic. These wicked monarchs spawned children who executed especially evil exploits in their own right.

Ahab and Jezebel had more than a quiver full of children. Scripture describes three of them—Athaliah, Ahaziah, and Jehoram—in some detail. When you study their lives, the evil parental influence is not difficult to discern from a natural perspective. But there's more to it than that. In Numbers 14:18 Jehovah vows to visit the iniquity of the fathers on the children to the third and fourth generations. It doesn't take a prophet to see the generational curses stemming from idolatry and immorality—and even murder—passed down this family line. But let me connect the dots for you anyway.

Maybe you've met some of the children of Jezebel and Ahab. These people aren't flowing in a full-blown Jezebel or Ahab spirit but have taken on some of their tendencies, hence, "like mother, like daughter," and "like father, like son." The daughter is not the mother and the son is not the father, but you might mistake one for another at a distance. They may sound the same, have similar gestures or facial expressions, look a lot alike, and even walk with the same gait.

Like natural-born children, Jezebel and Ahab's spiritual children start off depending on their demonic spiritual parents to teach them the ways of the world. But, like rebellious teenagers, these spiritual offspring soon emerge as independent and develop evil agendas uniquely their own. The spiritual children of Jezebel and Ahab are so dangerous, in part, because they tend to be even more wicked than their parents. It's as if they have something to prove.

Think about it for a minute, Ahab was worse than his father, Omri. The Bible says he did more to provoke the Lord to anger than all the kings of Israel who ruled before him (1 Kings 16:33). Likewise, we know Solomon made the people's yoke heavy but that his son, Rehoboam, ruled with such a hard fist that Israel revolted against him (1 Kings 12). And it was Jeremiah who prophesied these words of the Lord to Israel: "And you have done worse than your fathers, for here you are, each one walking after the imaginations of his evil heart so that they do not listen to Me" (Jer. 16:12).

We need to be cautious of Jezebel and Ahab, but not only Jezebel and Ahab. We also need to be vigilant concerning the plots and schemes of their children—or spiritual children, as it were. The spiritual spawn of Jezebel and Ahab are uniquely evil because they can take on the characteristics of both spirits. So while it can be difficult to discern, based on appearances, whether you're dealing with a Jezebel or an Athaliah, it's even more difficult to solve the spiritual equation if the spiritual son or daughter has been raised by spiritual parents operating in Ahab and Jezebel. Confusing the matter even more, Christians who sit under a ministry where Jezebel or Ahab rules can take on the characteristics of Jezebel or Ahab even if they aren't flowing in a full-blown Jezebel spirit.

Only the Holy Spirit can give you the answers you ultimately need to put together the demonic puzzle pieces, resist these devils, and watch them flee. However, it's wise not to be ignorant of the enemy's devices, so that when the Holy Spirit quickens your spirit to the presence of these demons you'll be equipped to cast them out and overcome them. In this chapter we'll discuss how Jezebel propagates spiritual children, what motivates them, how to recognize these Jezebelites, and how to avoid becoming one.

All About Athaliah

Jezebel and Ahab had many children. One of them was Athaliah, the queen of Judah. Different from eunuchs, Jezebel's children are higher ranking in its demonic kingdom. The spirit of Athaliah is somewhat like Jezebel's "Mini-Me"—a smaller version, but an otherwise carbon copy. She learned from her mother's wicked ways, destroying all the royal heirs (except one who was rescued from her evil grip) in order to take the throne of Judah.

Remember, *Smith's Bible Dictionary* defines Athaliah as "afflicted of the Lord" and *Easton's Bible Dictionary* defines the name as "whom God afflicts."[1] It's an appropriate name for the daughter of the wicked Queen Jezebel. Athaliah came from the royal line of Omri, the sixth king of Israel. Her parents sought out political alliances through marriage to advance their kingdom, and Athaliah was given to Jehoram, the eldest son of Judah's King Jehoshaphat (2 Kings 8:18). Athaliah actually murdered her own grandchildren (2 Chron. 22:11), outdoing the evil of her own mother.

What does the spirit of Athaliah look like in action? This is a murdering, self-advancing spirit—much like Jezebel.

Athaliah's son was Ahaziah. He became king of Judah when he was twenty-two years old but reigned only one year (2 Kings 8:25–26). The Bible says, "He walked in the way of the house of Ahab and did evil in the sight of the LORD, as the house of Ahab did, for he was the son-in-law of the house of Ahab" (v. 27).

When Jehu killed Ahab's family, which included Ahaziah (2 Kings 10), Athaliah rose up and destroyed all but one of the royal heirs. This was barbarous at best. Athaliah was not only a murderess but also by definition a serial murderess who surpassed the wickedness of her mother. Jezebel had the prophets of God murdered, but Athaliah—both a queen's daughter and a king's wife—murdered her own royal flesh and blood.

What was her motive? Power. *Matthew Henry's*

Commentary puts it this way: "She thirsted after rule and thought she could not get to it any other way. That none might reign with her, she slew even the infants and sucklings that might have reigned after her. For fear of a competitor, not any must be reserved for a successor."[2] Athaliah got her way. According to 2 Kings 11:3, she ruled over the land.

Athaliah's Brothers Are No Better

Two of Athaliah's named brothers in Scripture were no better than the wicked Queen Jezebel. One of them was Ahaziah. According to *Easton's Bible Dictionary*, his name means "held by Jehovah."[3] But his good name did not produce good character. He took after characteristics of Ahab but was clearly also influenced by his evil mother.

Ahaziah was the eighth king of Israel, actually succeeding Ahab after he was killed in battle. It's obvious Jezebel taught him to worship Baal and Ashtoreth rather than loving Jehovah with all his heart, all his mind, and all his strength. When he was sick, he consulted with false gods for counsel instead of turning his heart to God (2 Kings 1:2). Elijah met Ahaziah with a prophetic word not unlike what he delivered to his father, Ahab. Jezebel's children may turn to Jehovah, but it's not the first or only place they turn in time of trouble

> Ahaziah fell down through a lattice in his upper chamber that was in Samaria and became ill. So he sent messengers and said to them, "Go, inquire of Baal-Zebub the god of Ekron whether I will recover from this illness." But the angel of the

> LORD said to Elijah the Tishbite, "Arise, go up to meet the messengers of the king of Samaria, and say to them, 'Is it because there is not a God in Israel, that you go to inquire of Baal-Zebub the god of Ekron?' Therefore thus says the LORD, 'You will not come down from the bed on which you have gone up but will surely die.'" Then Elijah departed.
>
> —2 KINGS 1:2–4

Elijah's words did not fall to the ground. Ahaziah died according to the word of the Lord. But his brother Jehoram remained. He was king of the northern kingdom of Israel and ruled twelve years (2 Kings 3:1). Although *Smith's Bible Dictionary* defines his name as "whom Jehovah has exalted" and *Hitchcock's Bible Names Dictionary* defines Jehoram as "exaltation of the Lord,"[4] he did not live up to his name. Indeed, Jezebel taught him to worship Baal.

At one point Elisha tried to help Jehoram by revealing Syria's battle plans, but Jehoram later turned on the man of God and actually vowed to kill him just as Jezebel threatened to kill Elijah (2 Kings 6:31). Like mother, like son. Elisha called him "the son of a murderer" (v. 32) after Jehoram cursed him with these words: "So may God do to me, and even more, if the head of Elisha the son of Shaphat stands on his shoulders after today" (v. 31). Sound familiar? That was almost a carbon copy of the curse Jezebel issued against Elijah after he executed her false prophets.

Jezebel's grandchildren are also portrayed as evildoers in Scripture: "For the sons of Athaliah, the wicked woman, had broken into the house of God and even used all the holy items of the house of the LORD for Baal worship" (2 Chron. 24:7). The point is that the family line of Ahab and Jezebel is perverted. Not one good person rose from the bunch. None of them served the Lord. None appreciated the true prophetic gift. None had integrity in the end. No, not one.

How Jezebel and Ahab Birth Spiritual Children

With companies of young prophets rising up and armies of prophetic believers awakening to establish the kingdom of God in the earth, spiritual guidance is vital to building a stable church that an unstable world will look to for answers. Jezebel wants young prophets to eat at her table. She wants to pervert prophetic voices for use in her false kingdom. Ahab is willing to foot the bill for this discipleship so he can surround himself with yes-men who tell him what he wants to hear even when it will get him killed. But it's not just prophets. Jezebel and Ahab want spiritual children who will help forward their agenda in the earth no matter what gifts they carry.

So how do Jezebel and Ahab birth spiritual children? In a manner similar to the way true spiritual mothers and fathers birth spiritual children, but with a perverted twist. True spiritual mothers, for example, see the gift of God in a person and feel drawn to disciple that person with a mix of God's love and truth and their own practical insight. People operating in a Jezebel spirit add spiritual children to the puppet show by identifying the hurts and wounds in a person and manipulating them with a warped take on God's love and truth, mixed with demonic insight. Ahab works the same way.

Much like the spirit of Jezebel targets wounded souls and influences their thought lives, those operating in the Jezebel spirit target wounded souls to mentor and disciple. Again, Jezebel's children aren't necessarily operating in a full-blown demonic spirit, but if they give themselves over to the ways of their mother long enough—and if they stay in Jezebel's incubator long enough—they will eventually carry the same spirit. Again, Ahab works the same way. It's important to note that Jezebel can have spiritual sons and Ahab can have spiritual daughters. In other words, men can flow in a Jezebel spirit and women can flow in an Ahab spirit.

Be careful whom you let speak into your life. People operating in Jezebel and Ahab spirits are power hungry and seek disciples who can help them overthrow righteous authority and replace it with corrupt spiritual government. Some church splits, I believe, start with Jezebels and Ahabs birthing spiritual children who rise up in a revolt against righteous leadership and cause churches to come apart at the seams. Sometimes that looks like a church split. Sometimes the church crumbles and falls, like a house divided against itself that can't stand (Mark 3:25).

Jezebel's children (and Ahab's children) are motivated by the same drivers that spur their wicked parents: power and control. They aren't willing to humble themselves and let God exalt them in due time (1 Pet. 5:6). They want to exalt themselves in their own timing. They are impatient, aggressive, and, again, often more wicked in deed than the parents who birthed them. Remember, Athaliah actually murdered her own grandchildren so she wouldn't have to share the throne with anyone. She wanted ultimate power and shunned righteous authority that got in her way—even babies in her own royal family line.

So how do you recognize the offspring of Jezebel and Ahab? You probably won't recognize them on the surface. Like Jezebel and Ahab, these wicked spiritual children often wear masks. There's no laundry list of traits you can check off like an online survey that shows you how likely someone is to be an Athaliah or a Jehoram. It's important that you know Jezebel has spiritual children so that your eyes are open to the devil's devices, which makes it easier for the Holy Spirit to break in with light about what may be operating against you.

That said, look for the fruit that we keep discussing as a warning sign and an impetus to pray. What Jesus said about false prophets applies equally to the children of Jezebel and Ahab: "Beware of false prophets who come to you in sheep's clothing, but inwardly they are ravenous wolves. You will know them by their fruit. Do men gather grapes from thorns, or figs from thistles? Even so, every good tree bears good fruit. But a corrupt tree bears evil fruit. A good tree cannot bear evil fruit, nor can a corrupt tree bear good fruit. Every tree that does not bear good fruit is cut down and thrown into the fire. Therefore, by their fruit you will know them" (Matt. 7:15–20).

"I Will Put Her Children to Death"

Jesus stands against Jezebel's children with the same zeal with which He stands against Jezebel. Although Jezebel's children can surely repent (a topic we'll explore in the next chapter), if they refuse to break ties with Jezebel, resist this spirit's flattering promises, and submit to the Lordship of Jesus Christ and the authority He has set up in the earth, it won't turn out too well for them.

Jesus meant what He said: "I will put her children to death, and all the churches shall know that I am He who searches the hearts and minds" (Rev. 2:23). Of course, Jezebel's children won't go down without a fight. Again, like mother, like daughter.

When Queen Jezebel saw the writing on the wall, she thought she could seduce, lie, and intimidate her way out of her fate. Consider the encounter between Jehu and Jezebel: "When Jehu came to Jezreel, Jezebel heard about it. She put black paint on her eyes, adorned her head, and looked down through the window. As Jehu entered in at the gate, she said, "Is everything all right, Zimri, murderer of his master?" (2 Kings 9:30–31).

Jezebel painted her face and adorned her head—she was trying to seduce Jehu as she looked down on him through the window if perchance he might fall into her trap and make her queen again. When that didn't work, she made false accusations against Jehu, comparing him to Zimri, who conspired against King Asa of Judah to murder him and take the throne. Zimri killed Asa and reigned (1 Kings 16:8–10).

Athaliah may have been watching in the wings as her mother tried to work her witchcraft on Jehu. Although it clearly did not work—Jehu called for the eunuchs to throw her down and they did—Athaliah employed a similar tactic when she faced her executioner. Here's the scene. Athaliah had just lost the throne as one of the king's sons, Joash, who survived her slaughter was anointed and crowned king:

> Now when Athaliah heard the noise of the escorts and the people, she came to the people in the temple of the LORD. When she looked, there was the king standing by a pillar according to custom; and the leaders and the trumpeters were by the king. All the people of the land were rejoicing and blowing trumpets. So Athaliah tore her clothes and cried out, "Treason! Treason!" And Jehoiada the priest commanded the captains of the hundreds, the officers of the army, and said to them, "Take her outside under guard, and slay with the sword whoever follows her." For the priest had said, "Do not let her be killed in the house of the LORD."
>
> —2 KINGS 11:13–15, NKJV

Can you see the similarity? Just as Jezebel accused Jehu of treason, Athaliah accused the officers of the army of treason. Just as Jehu the king called for the eunuchs to throw Jezebel down, Jehoiada, the king's priest, called for the officers to slay Athaliah. And just as Jesus said He would kill Jezebel's children, the priest called the officers to kill all of Athaliah's followers. If you are following Jezebel or Athaliah, you are setting yourself up for a slow spiritual death. You need to get out of Jezebel's family and see yourself as a son or daughter of God. He's waiting.

How to Get Out of Jezebel's Family

So how do you get out of Jezebel's family? You need to repent, but you may also need the help of true, godly spiritual parents to get your life back on track. For all the accurate prophetic decrees and miraculous moments that characterized Elijah's ministry, it is his spiritual fatherhood that is perhaps most needed in the body of Christ today. As we consider Elijah and his miraculous ministry, let us also consider this powerful prophet's role in shaping the life and ministry of young Elisha, who went on to do far greater things than his spiritual mentor.

Many in this generation crave the input of spiritual mothers and fathers. Jezebel and Ahab know this and will seek out those who are not being nurtured by genuine, well-intended spiritual mentors. The manifestation of the sons of God depends on spiritual parents who will invest time and energy into their spiritual children. Breaking free from Jezebel's family demands a manifestation of Malachi 4:6: "He will turn the hearts of the fathers to their children, and the hearts of the children to their fathers, lest I come and strike the earth with a curse."

Unfortunately there's a lack of spiritual fathers and mothers, which has opened the door for Jezebels and Ahabs to step in. Many of today's local church leaders were not fathered themselves, and subsequently do not know how to father others. Characteristics of a true spiritual father or mother include protection, guidance, instruction, correction, exhortation, encouragement, and inspiration. Spiritual parents share life lessons, anchor their children in character and purpose, and give them opportunities to express their gifts and talents in a healthy environment.

Despite this lack of spiritual fathers and mothers, there is a move afoot in the body of Christ among mature believers to step in as mentors in this hour. But Jezebel's children must still be willing sons and daughters of godly leadership to truly find lasting deliverance. An independent spirit often causes would-be sons to resist sonship, most notably the correction that comes with the relationship. However, fathers who refuse to correct their sons will lose their sons as Eli lost his (1 Sam. 2:34, 4:11). And the Bible clearly states that those who will not receive correction will become bastards (Heb. 12:8).

Anybody can receive Jezebel's words of flattery, but how do you receive the Father's words of discipline through the mouth of a spiritual mentor? If you want to break free from Jezebel's family, you need to shun flattery and receive godly encouragement—and, at times, godly correction. Just as we honor God by asking Him to help us with our challenges, spiritual sons honor their spiritual fathers by asking them for insight. The establishment of the kingdom demands spiritual fathers who are willing to propel their spiritual sons to greater heights. And breaking free from Jezebel's family demands spiritual sons and daughters who are willing to take wise counsel from true fathers and mothers.

If you find yourself in a position to minister to a soul that has been influenced by Jezebel or Ahab, proceed with caution and stay close to the Holy Spirit. Although you have nothing to fear from these spirits that have infiltrated their souls, you do need to be cautious that they don't look to your mentorship in an ungodly way, forming new soul ties with you as they had with Jezebel. People trying to escape Jezebel's clutches are especially vulnerable because their identities and loyalties have been displaced. This is not as much about casting out devils as it is truly parenting the soul to bring healing that shuts the door once and for all on the spirits that sought out their woundedness.

In the next chapter we'll explore more in-depth what true repentance really looks like and how to recognize the false repentance of Jezebel and her children.

Chapter 11

GIVING JEZEBEL (AND HER CHILDREN) SPACE TO REPENT

NOW THAT WE'VE seen the fate of Queen Jezebel's natural children, let's flip ahead to the Book of Revelation and explore in depth the fate of the false prophetess Jezebel's spiritual children—and all those who commit adultery with her. You'll discover a parallel worth noting and what I consider biblical evidence that the spirit we call Jezebel is the same spirit that was working through both Queen Jezebel and the false prophetess Jezebel. Although the Book of Revelation doesn't explicitly offer a picture of the false prophetess's downfall, we do know that she refused to repent, like the queen who carried the same name (and the same spirit).

Let's look again at Revelation 2:

> To the angel of the church in Thyatira write: "he Son of God, who has eyes like a flame of fire, and whose feet are like fine brass, says these things: I know your works, love, service, faith, and your patience, and that your last works are more than the first. But I have a few things against you: You permit that woman Jezebel, who calls herself a prophetess, to teach and seduce My servants to commit sexual immorality and eat food sacrificed to idols. I gave her time to repent of her sexual immorality, but she did not repent. Look! I will throw her onto a sickbed, and those who commit adultery with her into great tribulation, unless they repent of their deeds. I will put her children to death, and all the churches shall know that I am He who searches the hearts and minds. I will give to each one of you according to your deeds."
>
> —Revelation 2:18–23

All I can say is, *Whoa!* Or should I say, "Woe!"? That's at least as bad, if not worse, than the woes Jesus pronounced on the religious Pharisees in Matthew 23! Let's take some time to unpack these judgments so we can see what is truly going to happen to Jezebel and those who bow to its false gods. First, it's important to note that Jesus gave Jezebel space to repent. This is God's way—always. As the palmist put it, "The Lord is merciful and gracious, slow to anger, and abounding in mercy" (Ps. 103:8).

Let me say this before we go any further: any time we discern that someone is operating in a Jezebel spirit, our first response should be to pity the person because he is in bondage to an evil that could have eternal consequences for him. That doesn't mean we tolerate the Jezebel spirit working through that individual, but we need to be mindful to separate the principality from the personality.

Although it's possible the Jezebel spirit's host has given himself over to this spirit's influence in his life knowingly, Jezebel more often enters through hurts and wounds that afflicted the person's soul through no fault of his own. He was merely unequipped to fend off the opportunistic demons looking for a vessel through which to operate. Our prayer is that the person is set free from Jezebel, so we pray for the person but refuse to tolerate the behavior. The goal is to facilitate true repentance. But Ahab manifests false repentance, and Jezebel simply won't repent—and doesn't want its puppets to either.

What Does It Really Mean to Repent?

God sent Elijah to Ahab with a prophetic word of judgment. Ahab sure looked repentant, but we see no change of heart. Let's look at the scene. Elijah prophesied:

> "See, I will bring disaster upon you and will take away your posterity and will cut off all your males, both free and slave, who are left in Israel, and will make your house like the house of Jeroboam the son of Nebat and like the house of Baasha the son of Ahijah, for the provocation with which you have provoked Me to anger and made Israel to sin."
>
> The Lord also spoke of Jezebel, saying, "The dogs will eat Jezebel by the wall of Jezreel." Those from Ahab's family who die in the city will be

> eaten by dogs, and those who die in the field will be eaten by birds of the air.
>
> —1 KINGS 21:21–24

Ahab had to respond. He would either stiffen his neck or repent. His response looked good on the outside: "When Ahab heard those words, he tore his clothes and put on sackcloth on his flesh and fasted and lay in sackcloth and walked meekly" (1 Kings 21:27). The Lord took notice of his repentance: "The word of the LORD came to Elijah the Tishbite, saying, 'See how Ahab humbles himself before Me? Because he humbles himself before Me, I will not bring the disaster during his lifetime, but during his son's lifetime I will bring the disaster on his household'" (vv. 28–29).

Ahab's repentance didn't stick. Almost immediately he began seeking counsel from false prophets and persecuting true prophets (1 Kings 22). His repentance may have been heartfelt in that moment, but true repentance demands a heart change, not a heart feeling alone. The fact that he turned aside from his sackcloth and ashes to aligning with Jehoshaphat to go to battle—and ordering the prophet Micaiah put in prison for speaking the very words of the Lord—demonstrates that his repentance faltered, if it ever existed. Ahab's repentance seems more like religious repentance, perhaps even worldly sorrow. He never confessed his sin; he just reacted to God's judgment.

False repentance is just what it sounds like: false repentance. Someone pretends to repent in order to get back in good graces with you, but his mind and heart are not changed. He doesn't hate the sin. Before we look at how to discern false repentance, let's define the word *repent* as it relates to Jezebel. The Greek word for *repent* in Revelation 2:21 is *metanoeō*, which means "to change one's mind, i.e., to repent; to change one's mind for the better, heartily to amend with abhorrence of one's past sins."[1]

When John the Baptist preached, "Repent, for the kingdom of heaven is at hand" (Matt. 3:2), he meant *metanoeō*. When Jesus preached "Repent! For the kingdom of heaven is at hand" (Matt. 4:17), He meant *metanoeō*. Likewise, when Jesus rebuked the cities of Chorazin and Bethsaida for not repenting after they saw the mighty works He did (Matt. 11:20–21), He was referring to *metanoeō*. When Jesus told His disciples there would be more joy in heaven over a single sinner who repents than ninety-nine just persons who need no repentance (Luke 15:7), He was talking about *metanoeō*.

Jesus doesn't want us just to be sorry for our sin—or sorry that we were caught sinning, like the rebellious teenager who puts on a good show after he brings home bad grades, fails to meet curfew, or gets caught sneaking in drunk. Jesus wants us to change our minds for the better, to heartily amend our ways and to abhor—yes, abhor—our past sins. He wants us to be sincere in our repentance.

But Jezebel and Ahab repent falsely. They are like the brood of vipers John the Baptist rebuked. Picture the scene. John the Baptist was clothed in camel's hair and wearing a leather belt. He dined on locusts and honey in the wilderness for years. When he emerged from obscurity, he started saying: "'Repent, for the kingdom of heaven is at hand.' For this is he who was spoken of by the prophet Isaiah, saying: 'The voice of one crying in the wilderness: "Prepare the way of the Lord; make His paths straight"'" (Matt. 3:2–3).

John the Baptist caused quite a stir, so much so that the Bible says Jerusalem, all Judea, and all the region around the Jordan came out to see what the excitement was about. When they heard his Holy Spirit-inspired preaching, it pricked their hearts. They responded to his prophetic message and got baptized right then and there in the Jordan. They confessed their sins en masse. But when John the Baptist saw the Pharisees and Sadducees coming to the baptism—these are representatives of a legalistic, religious spirit—he wasted no time rebuking them:

> But when he saw many of the Pharisees and Sadducees come to his baptism, he said to them, "O generation of vipers, who has warned you to escape from the wrath to come? Therefore, bear fruit worthy of repentance, and do not think to say within yourselves, 'We have Abraham as our father,' for I say to you that God is able from these stones to raise up children for Abraham. Even now the axe is put to the tree roots. Therefore, every tree which does not bear good fruit is cut down and thrown into the fire. I indeed baptize you with water to repentance, but He who is coming after me is mightier than I, whose shoes I am not worthy to carry. He will baptize you with the Holy Spirit and with fire. His fan is in His hand, and He will thoroughly clean His floor and gather His wheat into the granary, but He will burn up the chaff with unquenchable fire."
>
> —MATTHEW 3:7–12

Discerning False Repentance

What a welcome! The point is that John wasn't going to baptize these men under the pretense of repentance. He discerned that they were not bearing fruits worthy of repentance. They were still walking in the pride of their heritage and status in society. John warned them, just as Jesus warned Jezebel, what would happen if they did not repent. We know that some of the Pharisees came to believe in the Lord, but others called for His death by crucifixion.

How do we discern whether repentance is true or false? Ultimately all discernment comes from the Holy Spirit. You can't guess if someone has repented, but you can judge the fruit even as you ask the Holy Spirit for discernment. It doesn't take much discernment to smell rotten fruit. Jesus said we would know false prophets by their fruit, and I believe we'll know false repentance by its fruit as well. Jesus said, "Even so, every good tree bears good fruit. But a corrupt tree bears evil fruit. A good tree cannot bear evil fruit, nor can a corrupt tree bear good fruit. Every tree that does not bear good fruit is cut down and thrown into the fire. Therefore, by their fruit you will know them" (Matt. 7:17–20).

Don't believe the fruit of a person's lips. Believe the fruit of his life. Believe his heart attitude about sin. A person may choose to stop engaging in certain behaviors that we call sin—such as drunkenness or fornication—but if he does not truly believe it is sin, then his heart and mind are wide open for the enemy to tempt him back into a snare. In other words, if he stopped sinning just to get the pastor off his back or just to keep his place on the praise team, it's not true repentance—it's false repentance, and backsliding is a real possibility. Listen to a person's words and watch his actions. Examine the fruit to see if true change is present. Behaviors don't change until the heart changes, and the heart doesn't change until the mind changes.

False repentance may come with tears—and even sackcloth and ashes. Pharaoh repented over and over to stop the plagues on Egypt, but he never intended in his heart to let the people go (Exod. 12:29–32). Balaam repented before the angel of the Lord but went on to teach Balak how to ensnare the Israelites (Num. 22:34). Esau repented for giving Jacob his birthright for a bowl of soup—repenting even with tears—but his sorrow was more for his own loss (Heb. 12:17).

False repentance has an outward manifestation, but there's no change of heart. Nineteenth century revivalist Charles Finney called it a sorrow for sin produced by worldly considerations and motives without regard to the true nature of sin. False repentance produces a shallow sorrow, not a godly sorrow. In 1836 Finney wrote:

> False repentance is founded in selfishness. It may be simply a strong feeling of regret, in the mind of the individual, that he has done, as he has, because he sees the evil consequences of it to himself, because it makes him miserable, or exposes him to the wrath of God, or injures his family or his friends, or because it produces some injury to himself in time or in eternity. All this is selfishness. He may feel remorse of conscience—biting, consuming REMORSE—and

> no true repentance. It may extend to fear—deep and dreadful fear—of the wrath of God and the pains of hell, and yet be purely selfish, and all the while there may be no such thing as a hearty abhorrence of sin, and no feelings of the heart going out after the convictions of the understanding, in regard to the infinite evil of sin.[2]

Discerning True Repentance

True repentance means a change of heart about the sin you've committed: seeing it the way God sees it, renouncing it, and turning away from it. Paul the Apostle breaks it down scripturally and contrasts worldly sorry with godly sorrow in a powerful way in 2 Corinthians 7:8–12:

> Though I caused you sorrow by my letter, I do not regret it, though I did regret it. For I perceive that this same letter has caused you sorrow, though only for a while. Now I rejoice, not that you were made sorrowful, but that your sorrow led to repentance. For you were made sorrowful in a godly way, that you might not suffer loss in any way through us. Godly sorrow produces repentance that leads to salvation and brings no regret, but the sorrow of the world produces death. For observe this very thing, which you sorrowed in a godly way: What carefulness it produced in you, what vindication of yourselves, what indignation, what fear, what intense desire, what zeal, what avenging of wrong! In all things you have proven yourselves to be innocent in this matter. So though I wrote to you, I did it not because of him who had done the wrong,

> nor because of him who suffered wrong, but that our care for you in the sight of God might be evident to you.

When I work in deliverance ministry, this is a Scripture we always read as we lead people toward freedom. In order to be truly free, one needs to see the truth about the behavior that led him into bondage the way God sees it. He has to develop a disgust for and a righteous indignation against the sin that allowed demon spirits to influence and oppress him. He has to take responsibility for his part and even understand how it hurt God's heart. This produces godly sorrow that produces repentance that sends demons running and invites the Holy Spirit to fill him to overflowing. Finney put it this way:

> To one who truly repents, sin looks like a very different thing from what it does to him who has not repented. Instead of looking like a thing that is desirable or fascinating, it looks the very opposite, most odious and detestable, and he is astonished at himself, that he ever could have desired such a thing. Impenitent sinners may look at sin and see that it will ruin them, because God will punish them for it; but, after all, it appears in itself desirable; they love it; they roll it under their tongue. If it could end in happiness, they never would think of abandoning it. But to the other it is different: he looks at his own conduct as perfectly hateful. He looks back on it, and exclaims, "How hateful, how detestable, how worthy of hell, such and such a thing was in me."[3]

David's repentance was not immediate after he committed adultery with Bathsheba and had her husband murdered to cover it up. But when David saw his sin, he absolutely turned his heart back to God. He wrote Psalm 51 after Nathan the prophet confronted him with the sin. You can read all nineteen verses in your Bible, but here's how the psalm starts: "Have mercy on me, O God, according to Your lovingkindness; according to the abundance of Your compassion, blot out my transgressions. Wash me thoroughly from my iniquity, and cleanse me from my sin" (Ps. 51:1–2).

Likewise, the prodigal son truly repented. The prodigal son asked for his inheritance and went off to a far country and wasted it all on wild living. After he ran out of money, a great famine hit the land, and he found himself starving and working as a hired hand feeding pigs. When he awakened to the reality of the consequences of his sin, he decided to set it right. "I will arise and go to my father, and I will say to him, 'Father, I have sinned against heaven and before you. I am no longer worthy to be called your son. Make me like one of your hired servants'" (Luke 15:18–19). This true repentance led to the prodigal son's reconciliation with his father. And so it is when we repent—we restore broken fellowship with the Father.

I Will Cast Her Onto a Sickbed

We read over and over in Scripture that the Lord is compassionate, gracious, slow to anger, abounding in mercy, and forgiving (Exod. 34:6; Num. 14:18; Ps. 86:15). God's patient kindness works to lead us to repentance (Rom. 2:4). Think about it for a minute: Jesus withheld

His judgment from Ahab and Jezebel for decades. Ahab reigned in Israel for thirty-two years. Jesus also gave the Jezebel of Revelation time to repent. But after she refused His grace, Jesus finally pronounced this judgment: "I will throw her onto a sickbed, and those who commit adultery with her into great tribulation, unless they repent of their deeds" (Rev. 2:22).

Barnes's commentary makes it clear. This is not a bed of ease but a bed of pain. "There is evidently a purpose to contrast this with her former condition. The harlot's bed and a sick-bed are thus brought together, as they are often, in fact, in the dispensations of Providence and the righteous judgments of God," Barnes writes. "One cannot be indulged without leading on, sooner or later, to the horrid sufferings of the other: and how soon no one knows."[4]

But it's not just Jezebel that will be cast onto a sickbed—it's those who commit adultery with this spirit. That means its followers and, I believe, also those who willfully tolerate the sin as Jezebel seduces people into immorality and idolatry. People who engage in the sins that Jezebel propagates will suffer Jezebel's fate if they don't repent.

Jesus gave Jezebel a space to repent. In his commentary Matthew Henry puts it this way: "Observe, first, repentance is necessary to prevent a sinner's ruin. Secondly, repentance requires time, a course of time, and time convenient; it is a great work, and a work of time. Thirdly, where God gives space for repentance, He expects fruits meet for repentance. Fourthly, where the space for repentance is lost, the sinner perishes with a double destruction. Jezebel doesn't want you to repent either."[5]

Jezebel Doesn't Want You to Repent

Jezebel would not repent—and it doesn't want you to, either. With regard to Jezebel, the late David Wilkerson put it this way: "I want to say, in no uncertain terms, that it is dangerous to sit under the wrong teaching. False doctrine can damn you more readily than all the lusts and sins of the flesh. False preachers and teachers are sending more people to hell than all the drug pushers, pimps and prostitutes combined. That is not an overstatement—I believe it. Multitudes of blind, misled Christians are singing and praising the Lord in churches enslaved by false doctrine. Thousands are sitting under teachers who are pouring out the doctrine of demons—and they come away saying, 'Wasn't that wonderful?'"[6]

David Wilkerson wrote those words in 1988 in relation to Jezebel's false doctrines. It has been twenty-five years since he sounded the alarm, and yet more believers today are being tossed to and fro by every wind of doctrine than ever before (Eph. 4:14). The Jezebel deception is real, whether you want to believe that a spirit of Jezebel exists or not. God's people are indeed selling out to Satan with a distorted message that is so staunchly defended by some that they work to publicly assassinate the character of anyone who speaks against it—labeling them Pharisees, legalists, and worse.

Make no mistake: I love the grace of God, but grace must stand on truth to be true grace.

Beloved, be not carried about with different and

strange doctrines (Heb. 13:9). Set your heart to endure sound doctrine rather than heaping up for yourself teachers who tickle your itching ears (2 Tim. 4:3). Stay true to the doctrine of Christ.

It's been said that the devil's greatest deception is convincing people he doesn't exist. If that's true, then Jezebel's greatest deception is convincing people she's all about control and manipulation while she's secretly, subtly perverting God's grace, seducing people away from repentance, even as a loving God is longing for them to repent.

If you need to repent, do it now and let it be from the heart; and produce the fruits of repentance. It's never too late.

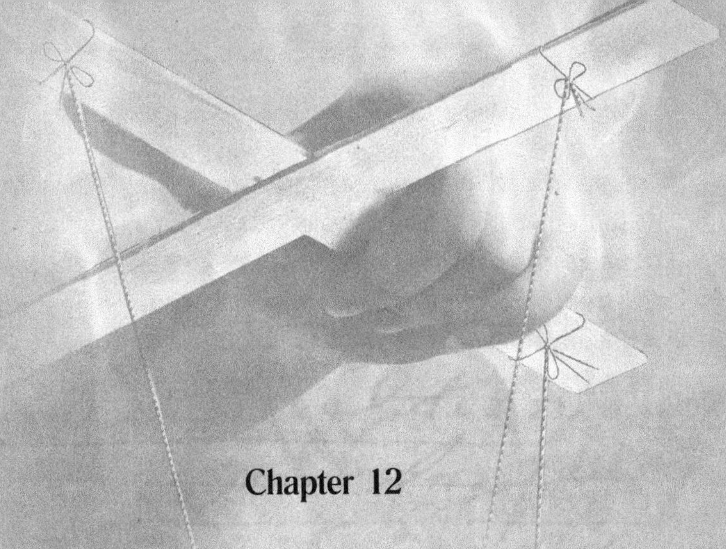

Chapter 12

OVERCOMING JEZEBEL'S OFFSPRING

LEAVING JEZEBEL'S HOUSE—REPENTING of giving in to this wicked spirit's influence and conquering the workings of this principality in your soul—doesn't mean Jezebel's offspring won't come after you. Jezebel's children lived on after the she met her fate with a pack of hungry dogs.

Indeed, even after you overcome Jezebel you may still have to deal with its spiritual offspring. I once left a church where Jezebel was ruling and reigning from the top down. Of course, there was only one so-called Jezebel. The other elders, deacons, prophets, and teachers were eunuchs and Jezebel's children.

For years I watched how Jezebel and her children verbally crucified people who left the church. I watched how Jezebel preached about them from the pulpit, subtly (and sometimes not so subtly) suggesting they were spies on assignment from the enemy, wolves in sheep's clothing, or too unstable to fight the good fight of faith. It always troubled me, and the fear of this persecution kept me in that church about two years longer than the Holy Spirit wanted me to stay.

What was interesting is that when I left this Jezebelic church, there was no confrontation with either Jezebel or Ahab. Ahab doesn't like confrontation, and Jezebel prefers to send her puppets to threaten you. Despite my long-term service to the church, these Jezebelic pastors did not meet with me. They did not ask me why I was leaving. Instead, they sent their eunuchs and spiritual children to make threats and false accusations against me, hoping to intimidate me back into my seat.

Here's what I believe the Lord showed me. There was no direct confrontation with the Jezebelic pastors because I had already conquered that spirit of Jezebel in my warfare. That warfare included: forgiveness for the spiritual abuse I endured, repentance for not leaving two years earlier, godly sorrow for allowing anyone other than the Holy Spirit to influence my behavior, breaking soul ties with the Jezebelic pastors, and engaging in ongoing spiritual battle over the Jezebel word curses that continued being spoken over my life until I felt the full release in the Spirit.

There was no direct confrontation with the Jezebelic pastors, but I still had to deal with Jezebel's children. They came at me from various angles, each with their own false accusations that aimed to bring me crawling back to the Jezebelic church for "deliverance" from Jezebel. Yes, it's ironic, but people under the influence of a Jezebel spirit will often accuse you of flowing in that spirit and offer to deliver you from it by the power of the God. What they are trying to do is strip you of your identity and wrap you up in their wicked web of deception.

Now let me take a quick rabbit trail to balance that out. Don't take these words as a license to ignore accusations that come against you. Ultimately you have to examine yourself and allow the Holy Spirit to show you if there is any wicked way in you. But if He has shown you plainly that you're sitting in a Jezebelic environment—whether that's a church, a workplace, or your home—you need to consider the source. It's also wise to seek outside counsel on the situation before moving on. Even if you do leave a Jezebelic church or workplace, it is likely you'll need the healing power of God to completely restore your soul after the spiritual stripping this spirit gives you.

Now back to the main thought. The good news is one anointing empowers you to conquer both Jezebel and its demonic spawn. It's the Jehu anointing. The Jehu anointing is different from the Elijah anointing, and you need this revelation to ultimately root out all traces of Jezebel and stand strong against the warfare these spirits bring against those who try to escape their clutches.

The Elijah anointing worked in miracles, sought repentance and revival for Israel, and ultimately confronted and conquered Jezebel's false prophets. But the Elijah anointing did not wipe out Jezebel or eradicate Ahab's house. However, I do believe these two anointings work together. Remember, Elijah was charged with anointing Jehu king over Israel before Jehu conquered Jezebel and Ahab's family line. It was ultimately Elisha's servant who actually anointed Jehu, but Elijah gave the order.

So who is this Jehu, and what kind of anointing did he have? Why was he able to face Jezebel's false accusations and overthrow the queen and her children after Elijah went running for the wilderness in fear that Jezebel would have his head? What can we learn from Jehu's warring spirit against idolatry that will help us recognize and battle attacks from Jezebel and her children? We'll answer those questions in this chapter.

Who Is This Jehu?

Elijah had failed to eradicate Jezebel's presence from the land. God needed a new man for this new hour to clean house. And it wasn't Elisha. It was Jehu. Indeed, Elijah defeated the false prophets, but Jehu overcame Jezebel and her offspring. From that we understand that it takes a different anointing—a different mind-set—to battle Jezebel's false prophetic puppets than it takes to combat Jezebel and her children.

Before we get into Jehu's fearless feats, let's get a better understanding of just who this warrior really was. Jehu was the son of Jehoshaphat and grandson of Nimshi (2 Kings 9:2). (Please note this is not the same Jehoshaphat who ruled as king over Judah.) Jehu set out in the footsteps of his fathers. The name *Nimshi* means "one who rescues those in danger," and that's just what Jehu did when he rid the kingdom of Israel of Ahab's family.

We first hear about Jehu after Elijah had an encounter with God that would shift the direction of his ministry. You remember the story from 1 Kings 18–19. Elijah called for a showdown with Jezebel's false prophets. The false prophets cried out to Baal until they lost their voices, but Baal was a no-show. When Elijah prayed to Jehovah, He immediately showed up and left no doubt who the living God really is. The Israelites turned their hearts toward God and against the false prophets. Elijah slew them in a mighty demonstration of authority but ran into the wilderness when Jezebel sent a messenger with a death threat.

Elijah sat in the wilderness under a broom tree praying that God would take his life before Jezebel got to him. Then he went to sleep before traveling forty days and nights to Horeb, the mountain of God (1 Kings 19:8). Elijah was still on the run from Jezebel. When God asked Him what he was doing at Horeb, Elijah told Jehovah all about his zeal and his woes. God then encountered him—but not with wind or earthquake or fire as Elijah was used to. It was with a still, small voice. In other words, God related to Elijah in a different way for a new season. But Elijah was still telling the same sad story:

> When Elijah heard it, he wrapped his face in his cloak and went out and stood in the entrance to the cave. And a voice came to him and said, "Why are you here, Elijah?" And he said, "I have been very zealous for the Lord, Lord of Hosts, because the children of Israel have forsaken Your covenant, thrown down Your altars, and killed your prophets with the sword, and I alone am left, and they seek to take my life."
>
> The Lord said to him, "Go, return on the road through the Wilderness of Damascus, and when you arrive, anoint Hazael to be king over Aram. And you shall anoint Jehu, the son of Nimshi, to be

> king over Israel, and you shall anoint Elisha, the son of Shaphat of Abel Meholah, to be prophet in your place. He who escapes the sword of Hazael will be killed by Jehu, and he who escapes the sword of Jehu will be killed by Elisha. Still, I have preserved seven thousand men in Israel for Myself, all of whose knees have not bowed to Baal and whose mouths have not kissed him."
>
> —1 Kings 19:13–18

Elijah obeyed. He called Elisha to follow him, and Elisha was a faithful servant until Elijah ascended to heaven and gave him a double portion of his anointing (2 Kings 2:9–12). At some point before Elijah went to glory, he instructed Elisha to anoint Jehu king over Israel. Elisha was waiting for just the right time; he clearly was led by the Holy Spirit. That time was after Jehoram, king of Israel, was wounded in a war against the Syrians in the battle at Ramoth Gilead. Jehoram, you will remember, was the son of Ahab and Jezebel. Jehoram's injury sparked a visit from his brother Ahaziah, the king of Judah (2 Kings 8:28–29). That opened the door for Jehu's anointing.

Jehu's Anointing

God called for Jehu to be anointed as king long before His perfect timing emerged, much like David was anointed king long before he took the throne. Can I take you on another quick rabbit trail? Your times are in God's hands. God could have put David on the throne sooner than He did. He was anointed for it. But David needed to go through the conflict with Saul and the wilderness times in order to gain the character he needed to lead a nation.

Much the same, Jehu was prophesied as Israel's next king long before he was anointed, but God needed to wait for circumstances to play out so Jehu would be received. Jehu was not from Ahab's family line—and that was the point. God needed a warrior to rise up with the authority to eradicate the bloodline of the man who did more to provoke Him than any other king before him (1 Kings 16:33). With two of Ahab's sons distracted, Elisha's servant found a window of opportunity to enter the army camp to anoint Jehu:

> Then Elisha the prophet called one of the sons of the prophets, "Prepare yourself. Take this flask of oil in your hand, and go to Ramoth Gilead. When you get there, look for Jehu the son of Jehoshaphat, the son of Nimshi. Go in and make him rise from among his brothers, and bring him into an inner chamber. Then take the flask of oil, pour it on his head, and say, 'Thus says the LORD: I have anointed you king over Israel.' Then open the door and flee. Do not wait."
>
> —2 KINGS 9:1–3

Elisha's servant obeyed and delivered a prophetic message to Jehu that, once obeyed, would remove the residue of Ahab and Jezebel from the kingdom of Israel and open the door to a revival in the land:

> So he arose, went into the house, poured the oil on his head, and said to him, "Thus says the LORD, God

> of Israel: I am anointing you king over the people of the LORD, over Israel. You will strike the house of Ahab your master, and I will avenge the blood of my servants the prophets and the blood of all the servants of the LORD from the hand of Jezebel. The whole house of Ahab will perish, and I will cut off from Ahab all the males in Israel, both imprisoned and free. I will make the house of Ahab like the house of Jeroboam son of Nebat and like the house of Baasha the son of Ahijah. Dogs will eat Jezebel in the territory of Jezreel, and no one will bury her." Then he opened the door and fled.
>
> —2 KINGS 9:6–10

What a word! Can you imagine? This is a strong example of intergenerational ministry. It took Jehu to fulfill Elijah's prophetic word. It took Elisha to carry the prophetic word from one generation to another. And it took Elisha's young servant to execute the command and physically anoint Jehu. So we see that God told Elijah to anoint Jehu but the instruction was actually fulfilled by Elisha's spiritual son. When God prophesies to you, you aren't always the one to carry out the word. Sometimes you are charged with equipping others to fulfill the word. Although Elijah didn't ultimately take down Jezebel, he was part and parcel of Jezebel's downfall and the desolation of Ahab's kingdom.

Jehu's head was probably spinning, but he had received an anointing to empower him to fulfill his mission—just as you've been given an anointing to empower you to fulfill your mission. If you are called to battle Jezebel, Ahab, and their children, God will give you the same anointing Elisha's servant poured out on Jehu. The Holy Spirit abides in you, and that's all the anointing you'll ever need, but the manifestation of that anointing will look like Jehu, which is why we call it the Jehu anointing.

Jehu didn't immediately accept the prophetic word. When Jehu emerged from this private anointing ceremony, the servants of his master asked him what happened. Jehu told them the young man was just babbling, but the servants weren't buying it. They demanded an answer from Jehu, and it took courage to respond: "Thus and thus he spoke to me, saying, 'Thus says the LORD: I am anointing you king over Israel'" (2 Kings 9:12). Jehu may not have been expecting what happened next: "Each took his clothes, put them under him on the bare stairs, and blew a horn, saying, 'Jehu is king'" (v. 13). From that moment Jehu set out to obey the prophecy.

JEHU'S FURIOUS CHARIOT OF JUDGMENT

Jehu wasted no time. He got in his chariot—his company following behind him—and drove furiously to Jezreel where Joram and Ahaziah, Jezebel's son, were staying. Along the way two of Joram's servants asked Jehu if he was coming in peace until finally he arrived in Jezreel and Joram asked him personally, "Is it peace, Jehu?" I love Jehu's answer: "What peace, as long as the harlotries of your mother Jezebel and her witchcraft are so many?" (v. 22, NKJV).

Joram launched a false accusation of treachery against Jehu, something he learned from his wicked mother, Jezebel, but that didn't stop Jehu from executing judgment. Jehu shot Joram between his arms with a bow and the arrow came out at his heart (v. 24). Jehu was not filled with the Holy Spirit, but he was careful to remember the prophetic words spoken over him and the house of Ahab and walk worthy of his newfound vocation as king of Israel to fulfill them. Jehu reminded his men of the prophetic word and offered an instruction:

> Then Jehu said to Bidkar his officer, "Lift him up and throw him on the property of the field of Naboth the Jezreelite. Remember when you and I were riding together after Ahab his father and the LORD pronounced this oracle about him: 'Surely I have seen yesterday the blood of Naboth and his sons, declares the LORD, and I will pay you back on this property, declares the Lord.' Now lift him up and throw him onto the property, according to the word of the LORD."
>
> —2 KINGS 9:25–26

Next Jehu went after Ahaziah as he was fleeing. Jehu ordered his men to shoot him as he was escaping in his chariot. Ahaziah fled to Megiddo and died there (v. 27). Then Jehu charged toward Jezebel's palace:

> When Jehu came to Jezreel, Jezebel heard about it. She put black paint on her eyes, adorned her head, and looked down through the window. As Jehu entered in at the gate, she said, "Is everything all right, Zimri, murderer of his master?"
>
> And he lifted up his face toward the window and said, "Who is on my side? Who?" And two or three eunuchs looked down to him. He said, "Drop her down." So they dropped her down and some of her blood splattered on the wall and on

> the horses. Then he trampled her. Then he entered, ate and drank, and said, "Attend to that cursed woman and bury her, for she is a king's daughter." So they went to bury her, but they found nothing of her except a skull, the feet, and the palms of her hands. They returned and told Jehu, and he said, "This is the word of the LORD, which He spoke by His servant Elijah the Tishbite, saying, 'On the property of Jezreel dogs will eat the flesh of Jezebel. The corpse of Jezebel will be like dung in the field on the property of Jezreel, so that they cannot say, This is Jezebel.'"
>
> —2 KINGS 9:30–37

How dramatic! One would think this would be enough satisfaction for anybody. But Jehu knew his work was not finished. He did not rest in the victory of defeating Jezebelic kings or Jezebel herself. Jehu would drive his chariot furiously to defeat the rest of her bloodline. He would defeat all of Jezebel's children. This is your mandate. Remember, even after you defeat Jezebel some of her children may be there to persecute and harass you. And remember, I'm not talking about actual people because we aren't wrestling against flesh and blood. But evil spirits can influence people without actually possessing them. If you are going to completely overcome Jezebel, you need to overcome her spiritual children in the sense that you rid your life of their influence over your soul.

JEHU PUTS AHAB'S SONS ON WARNING

Ahab had seventy sons in Samaria. Rather than rushing in furiously on his chariot as he did during his march into

Jezreel to dethrone the kings by death and throw down Jezebel, Jehu wrote letters to Jezreel's rulers and elders and those who were raising Ahab's sons. The letter said:

> Now as soon as this letter comes to you—since you are with your master's sons, chariots, horses, a fortified city, and weapons—select the best and most fitting of your master's sons, put him on his father's throne, and fight for your master's house.
>
> —2 Kings 10:2–3

The Jezreelites—even those charged to care for Ahab's sons—saw the writing on the wall. They fearfully declined to put one of Ahab's sons on the throne and told Jehu to do whatever he felt was right. He sent a second letter instructing them to meet him at Jezreel the next day with the heads of Ahab's seventy sons. Can you imagine the slaughter that evening? What a bloody end to a bloodline. The Jezreelites obeyed Jehu's command, and the next day Israel's anointed king addressed the people, reminding them once again of the prophetic word over Ahab's house:

> "You are innocent. I conspired against my master and killed him, but who struck all these? Know then that the words of the Lord which He spoke about the house of Ahab will not fall to the ground. The Lord has done that which He spoke by His servant Elijah." So Jehu struck all that remained of the house of Ahab in Jezreel and all his great men, his confidants, and his priests, until he left him no survivor.
>
> —2 Kings 10:9–11

From there Jehu went on to kill Ahaziah's forty-two brothers and the rest of Ahab's family (2 Kings 10:12–17). Put another way, Jehu killed Jezebel and all her puppets. As long as Jezebel's puppets remain, the show will go on. A new Jezebel—someone operating in a spirit of Jezebel—will emerge to orchestrate the show. Just because you rid your life of a person flowing in a spirit of Jezebel that's seeking to seduce you into idolatry and immorality doesn't mean that you've conquered Jezebel once and for all. You are likely to have more than one battle with this principality, especially if you carry a prophetic voice. Keeping Jezebel's children around makes it easier for Jezebel to find a way back in your life. You can't hang out with the kids without eventually running into the mother.

Jehu Blasts Baal Worship

Jehu saved the Baal worshippers for last. Although Israel claimed to have turned its heart back to God after Elijah's showdown with the false prophets, we know that false prophets continued to rise up in Ahab's kingdom, serving the Baals and acting as his yes-men. Jehu was crafty in killing the Baal worshippers, pretending he wanted to join in their false praise:

> Then Jehu gathered all the people and said to them, "Ahab served Baal a little, but Jehu will serve him much. Now call to me all the prophets of Baal, all his worshippers, and all his priests. Let none go unaccounted for, because I have a great sacrifice for Baal. All who are not accounted for will not live."
>
> —2 Kings 10:18–19

Jehu was taking a page from Elijah's prophetic playbook, calling for a showdown with the spirit of Baal. But he tricked them into thinking he would take up where Ahab left off, only with more blood on his hands than Ahab ever spilt. It worked. The Bible says all the Baal worshippers came out—every single one of them:

> They came into the house of Baal, and the house of Baal was full from one end to the other. He said to the one in charge of the wardrobe, "Bring out garments for all the worshippers of Baal." So he brought them garments. Then Jehu and Jehonadab the son of Rekab went into the house of Baal and said to the worshippers of Baal, "Search and see that there are no worshippers of the LORD here with you and only worshippers of Baal." Then they went to offer sacrifices and burnt offerings, but Jehu put eighty men outside and said, "If any of the men whom I have brought into your hands escapes, the one who lets him go will die in his place."
>
> —2 KINGS 10:21–24

As soon as the Baal worshippers made the burnt offering, Jehu gave the command to the guard and the captains to kill them—every single one of them. See, the Baal worshippers had absolutely no discernment. If they had been at all prophetic, they would have discerned Jehu's plot. Think about it for a minute: Jehu in his zeal had destroyed the house of Ahab as an instrument of God's judgment. Did they really think he would turn and worship Baal in the next breath?

Here's a lesson for you: if you are worshipping idols,

your discernment will be dull. Selah. Stop and think about that. You can pray for discernment day and night, but if you are serving idols night and day, you will find it difficult beyond God's mercy to discern the assignments against you. Consider the words of the psalmist:

> Their idols are silver and gold, the work of men's hands. They have mouths, but they cannot speak; eyes, but they cannot see; they have ears, but they cannot hear; noses, but they cannot smell; they have hands, but they cannot feel; feet, but they cannot walk; neither can they speak with their throat. Those who make them are like them; so is everyone who trusts in them.
>
> —Psalm 115:4–8

Jehu's men killed the Baal worshippers and threw them out. But they didn't stop there, either. They went into the temple's inner room, carried out the sacred pillars of Baal's temple, and burned them to ashes. They also broke down Baal's sacred pillar and destroyed it. And the Bible says, "Thus Jehu destroyed Baal from Israel" (2 Kings 10:28, NKJV).

Israel saw reformation and should have seen revival, but there's no revival without an awakening of the heart. Jehu was zealous and obedient. Sadly, Jehu would turn back to the same sins of Ahab and Jezebel that angered God. I call this the Jehu Syndrome. We'll discuss this—and ways to avoid it—in the next chapter.

Chapter 13

AVOIDING THE JEHU SYNDROME

No one is immune to becoming a puppet in Jezebel's twisted spiritual play—not even those who preach about, pray against, and prophesy the ultimate doom of Jezebel. I know because I watched some mighty spiritual warriors fall to this spirit without their ever understanding what led to their demise.

The company's CEO, Jeff, didn't start out as CEO. He was a mail clerk in the company when it launched thirty years ago. After growing up in an abusive home, Jeff never dreamed he could overcome his past and emerge as a business success. But his faith in God and his hard work paid off. When the founder retired, he dubbed Jeff, who had climbed the ranks in the company over the years, as the next CEO.

What really put Jeff on the founder's radar screen was his accurate prophetic insights and keen spiritual-warfare skills. The founder was convinced Jeff's spiritual gifts helped the company make some profitable decisions about personnel and new markets. Jeff even helped the founder navigate through a planned coup when the board tried to oust him for a new leader during an economic crisis. Jeff was like a Jehu, helping the founder clean house and install loyal staff. Jeff even raised up spiritual warriors who had what he called a "Jehu anointing," who came in every morning to pray before work.

When the founder retired, Jeff took the reins of the company with a special blessing. But his absolute power began to corrupt him absolutely. It started with a chink in his spiritual armor. All it takes is a chink. That chink was unresolved hurts and wounds from repeated rejection and abuse in his past. Suddenly Jeff's band of spiritual warriors—the mighty Jehus—were acting like the devils they were trying to cast out. Of course, most people around them didn't discern what was going on until it was too late.

Jeff appeared decisive on the outside, but he was insecure and indecisive on the inside. This CEO, like many who operate in insecurity, surrounded himself with yes-men who told him what he wanted to hear. Jeff's staff fed his fragile ego and helped him forward his business goals as best as they could in a dysfunctional corporate family. Although they saw his flaws, they believed in his vision and covered his blind spots.

Jeff's inner circle remained tight as the company grew, but one new employee, Sarah, quickly gained the confidence of the group and was allowed to see and hear what most others had no idea was going on behind closed doors. Sarah was privy not only to the fits of anger but also the dishonest financial practices, the sexual immorality, and the clear favoritism with salaries.

Sarah watched for months as these systemic problems started taking their toll on the company. Employees were resigning over sexual harassment and worse. Sincerely concerned about the health of the business and its reputation in the Christian community, Sarah shared her concerns with Jeff and was swiftly fired. She had unknowingly tapped right into his insecurities and fears (rather than covering up the sore spots) and paid the price.

Before long the problems began to manifest at more noticeable levels. The issues were no longer kept hush-hush behind closed doors or washed away as rumors coming from disgruntled employees. The company's product quality started slipping. Employee loyalty suffered. Profits slipped. The inner circle discerned a Jezebel spirit attacking and battled in prayer until they lost their voices, sort of like those false prophets at the Mount Carmel showdown with Elijah.

Finally, one of the men in the inner circle saw the writing on the wall—the company was failing—and he left to take a job in a healthier environment. The rest went down with the ship—and the CEO was completely convinced that Jezebel took him out. Yes, Jezebel took the company down, but it was through Jeff and his power-hungry inner circle. They never saw it coming because they were blinded in their own sin. Who was the real Jehu in this picture? Sarah, the woman who was brave enough to call out the sins of the CEO.

Like Jeff, who helped the company's founder overcome

an internal coup to oust him during the economic crisis and was rewarded with the CEO position, Jehu eradicated Jezebel, Ahab, and their offspring from the kingdom of Israel before taking the throne. But, like Jeff, the mighty warrior Jehu soon fell into some of Jezebel's sins. This chapter will spell out those sins, which I am calling the Jehu Syndrome, and instruct readers how to rise up in a Jehu anointing without falling to Jehu's error.

Avoiding Jehu's Sins

In the last chapter we learned about the Jehu anointing—and saw the fruits of it. Jehu obeyed God to carry out a campaign that wiped out Ahab, Jezebel, and their children. He was bold. He was zealous. He was indignant. He was swift. He was shrewd. But after his mission was accomplished—after he destroyed Baal from Israel—he backslid. There should have been a massive revival in Israel, but the spirit of Jezebel was still influencing the nation of Israel:

> But from the sins of Jeroboam son of Nebat, who caused Israel to sin, Jehu did not turn aside (that is, the golden calves that were in Bethel and Dan). And the LORD said to Jehu, "Because you have done well by doing what is right in My sight, and have done to the house of Ahab all that was in My heart, four generations of your sons will sit on the throne of Israel." But Jehu was not careful to walk in the law of the LORD God of Israel with all his heart. He did not turn aside from the sins of Jeroboam, who caused Israel to sin.
>
> —2 KINGS 10:29–31

What? How could that happen? Could it be possible that Jehu's motives for his righteous rampage were not so righteous after all? Could it be possible that he simply wanted the throne for himself and saw the opportunity to seize it in the name of God? Did he deceive himself into believing he could continue in the sins Ahab and Jezebel propagated without finding a similar fate? Matthew Henry wrote in his commentary:

> Jehu showed great care and zeal for rooting out a false religion, but in the true religion he cared not, took no heed to please God and do his duty. Those that are heedless, it is to be feared, are graceless. The people were also careless, therefore it is not strange that in those days the Lord began to cut Israel short. They were short in their duty to God, therefore God cut them short in their extent, wealth, and power.[1]

But there's another issue here. Jehu went beyond the boundaries of God's prophetic word to him. Jehu fell into the ditch of excess—into extremism. Let's look again at the mandate God gave Jehu: "You will strike the house of Ahab your master, and I will avenge the blood of my servants the prophets and the blood of all the servants of the LORD from the hand of Jezebel. The whole house of Ahab will perish, and I will cut off from Ahab all the males in Israel, both imprisoned and free" (2 Kings 9:7–8).

It seems Jehu was a little too bloodthirsty for God's taste in his haste to take the throne. The Lord had commissioned him to kill "all who remained of the house of Ahab in Jezreel," but Jehu also killed Ahab's nobles, friends, and priests, "until he left him none remaining" (2 Kings 10:11, NKJV). Jehu was supposed to do away with Ahab and his family line, according to 2 Kings 10:30, but he was not told to go after Ahab's friends and priests.

God later told the prophet Hosea to take a harlot as a wife during a time when Israel was committing spiritual adultery. Hosea married Gomer, and they had a son. The Lord said to him: "Call his name Jezreel, for in a little while, I will punish the house of Jehu for the blood of Jezreel, and will bring to an end the kingdom of the house of Israel. On that day, I will break the bow of Israel in the Valley of Jezreel" (Hosea 1:4–5).

Although there are varying opinions on whether the bloodshed of Jezreel relates to Jehu's crusade against the house of Ahab or his subsequent tolerance of Jezebel's gods, it seems clear that Jehu's error was ultimately disobedience to God. Israel paid the price, and so did Jehu:

> In those days the LORD began to trim off parts of Israel, and Hazael struck them in all the territory of Israel: from the Jordan eastward, all the land of Gilead, the Gadites, the Reubenites, the Manassites from Aroer, which is by the River Arnon, even Gilead and Bashan. Now the rest of the deeds of Jehu, all he did and all his power, are they not written in the book of the annals of the kings of Israel? So Jehu slept with his fathers, and they buried him in Samaria. Jehoahaz his son became king in his place. The days that Jehu reigned over Israel in Samaria were twenty-eight years.
>
> —2 KINGS 10:32–36

There Is No Revival in Jezebel

So we learn from Jehu that even those who set out to rid the land—or the church or the workplace—of Jezebel and Ahab can quickly fall into the sins they claimed to hate. Yet there is a remnant. As ironic as it may sound, Queen Jezebel's great-grandson brought reformation to Judah.

Remember Jezebel's daughter Athaliah? When Jehu came storming through on his rampage and killed her son, King Ahaziah, she rose up and destroyed all the royal heirs hoping to take the throne for herself. But God preserved a seed from that wicked family line with redemption in mind:

> Now when Athaliah the mother of Ahaziah saw that her son was dead, she rose up and destroyed all the royal descendants. But Jehosheba, the daughter of King Joram, sister of Ahaziah, took Joash the son of Ahaziah, and stole him away from among the king's sons who were being murdered; and they hid him and his nurse in the bedroom, from Athaliah, so that he was not killed.
>
> —2 Kings 11:1–2

Judah crowned Joash king when he was only seven years old. Unlike his great-grandparents and his parents, he did what was right in the sight of the Lord, as Jehoiada the priest instructed him, the Bible says. During the early days of his reign the high places where people sacrificed to idols and burned incense were still up and running. Joash set out to correct that by repairing the temple, but he had to press through resistance from, of all people, the Levites:

> So the king called Jehoiada, who was head over this, and said to him, "Why have you not required from the Levites that they bring in from Judah and Jerusalem the tax levied by Moses, the servant of the LORD, for the congregation of Israel for the tent of the testimony?" For the sons of Athaliah, the wicked woman, had broken into the house of God and even used all the holy items of the house of the LORD for Baal worship.
>
> —2 CHRONICLES 24:6–7

Joash completed his mission, and there were burnt offerings in the house of the Lord continually during the days of Jehoiada (2 Chron. 24:14). Could it be possible that one from Jezebel's bloodline could drive true reformation in Israel? It was as close as the nation came, but when Jehoiada passed away—when the man of God was no longer guiding the king with godly wisdom—Joash rose up in the same spirit of his great-grandmother and turned away from the Lord. Even in Joash's apostasy we see our merciful God trying to redeem the situation.

JOASH SHOWS HIS JEZEBELIC ROOTS

> After the death of Jehoiada the officials of Judah came and paid homage to the king. At that time the king listened to them. Then they abandoned the house of the LORD and God of their fathers, and they served the Asherah poles and idols. And divine wrath was on Judah and Jerusalem because

> of this guilt. And *God* sent prophets to return them to the LORD. These warned the people, but they would not listen.
>
> Then the Spirit of God clothed Zechariah the son of Jehoiada the priest, and he stood above the people saying, "Thus says God: Why are you transgressing the commandments of the LORD so that you all will not be successful? Because you all have abandoned the LORD, He has abandoned you." But they plotted against him, and at the command of the king they all stoned him in the court of the house of the LORD. And Joash the king did not remember the kindness that Jehoiada the father of Zechariah had shown him, but killed his son. As he was dying, he said, "May the LORD see and avenge!"
>
> —2 CHRONICLES 24:17–22

And so Joash tempted the Lord in a manner similar to Jezebel. He cut off the voice of the true prophets and essentially dared God to deal with him. And God did. That spring the Syrian army came against Joash and destroyed all the leaders. In the end, just like Jezebel's eunuchs threw her down, Joash's servants conspired against him.

Betrayal

> For the army of the Syrians came with a small company of men; but the LORD delivered a very great army into their hand, because they had forsaken the LORD God of their fathers. So they executed judgment against Joash. And when they had withdrawn from him (for they left him severely wounded), his own servants conspired against him because of the blood of the sons of Jehoiada the

> priest, and killed him on his bed. So he died. And they buried him in the City of David, but they did not bury him in the tombs of the kings.
>
> —2 Chronicles 24:24–25, NKJV

And so the spirit of Jezebel continued to influence God's people. The lesson here is this: no one who has anything to do with Jezebel will ultimately lead you toward God unless there is true repentance. A Jezebelite may appear to be leading you in a godly way, but as long as the root of idol worship and immorality remains in his heart, danger is present—the spirit of Jezebel is alive and well. We saw it influence generations after Jehu conquered the wicked queen. It can still find a way to influence those who once conquered it, and it is still influencing generation after generation today.

Walking free and staying free from Jezebel and its puppets means walking with the Holy Spirit, communing with the Father, and putting on Christ. Anything that draws our hearts away from Him will leave us open to Jezebel's influence. With that said, this battle with Jezebel demands balance. If you start looking for Jezebel everywhere, you'll see Jezebel everywhere—even when it's not Jezebel. In other words, don't go on a witch hunt for these spirits. Let the Holy Spirit open your eyes to the spiritual warfare around you and walk in confidence that you have authority over Jezebel and its puppets.

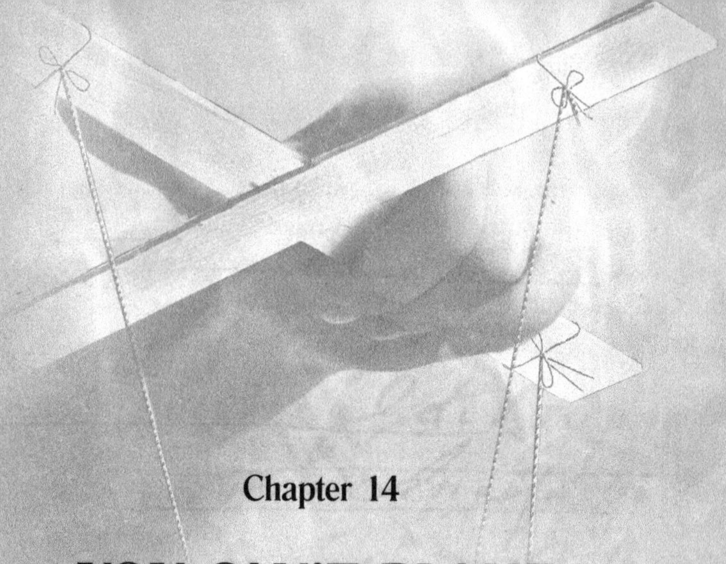

Chapter 14

YOU CAN'T BLAME EVERYTHING ON JEZEBEL

WHEN I FIRST got the revelation there was a demon spiritual warriors call Jezebel—and that it is roaming around like a roaring lion trying to destroy my purpose with its seductive, murderous agenda—my jaw literally dropped. In the light of this unveiling, Jezebel's subtle (and blatant) attacks against me over the years became easily discernable. Jezebel was an old enemy that I had never identified—until that revelation came.

As I began to study this spirit, I thought I saw it behind every doorknob, every bush, and every pew. Every time something went wrong in my life, I thought surely it must be this old enemy that I had never known was trying to turn my attention from Jesus and silence my voice. But I was wrong. Although the Jezebel spirit is alive and well, we can't blame everything on Jezebel.

In fact, that's a dangerous stance because if you're hyper-focused on Jezebel when Jezebel isn't attacking, then you could be overlooking the true culprit behind the scenes that is organizing the onslaught against you. We like to quote 1 Peter 5:8 in spiritual-warfare circles, but the Amplified Bible really brings out the Greek in a way that sheds light on an important spiritual-warfare principle—balance:

> Be sober [well balanced and self-disciplined], be alert and cautious at all times. That enemy of yours, the devil, prowls around like a roaring lion [fiercely hungry], seeking someone to devour. But resist him, be firm in your faith [against his attack—rooted, established, immovable], knowing that the same experiences of suffering are being experienced by your brothers and sisters throughout the world.
>
> —1 PETER 5:8–9, AMP

So, yes, by all means we should be vigilant and cautious at all times—we should be on the offense rather than the defense. And, yes, by all means we should understand that the enemy is real and guard our hearts and minds against the attacks. But if we have a pet demon we like to blame everything on, we're out of balance. If we assume the "spirit of the week" we hear about in popular books, magazines, and sermons is on our trail, we'll often wind up buffeting the air and opening ourselves up for a blind-side from the true demonic offender.

We Don't Know What We Don't Know

Let's not be wise in our own eyes but rather lean and depend on the Lord to discern what is coming against us. It's been said we don't know what we don't know, but it's just as true that we can't see what we can't see. Sometimes the enemy has so clouded our vision that we need God to break in with light—to open our eyes wide so we can see the supernatural events unfolding behind the natural scenes.

I've been there, and so have Balaam and Elisha's servant. Although we walk by faith and not by sight (2 Cor. 5:7), sometimes God will choose to let us see something supernatural to bolster our faith—or just to get our attention when we're going astray. Like I said, I've been there.

When God opens our eyes, it may be in the form of a prophetic dream, a vision, a trance, or even what feels like a real-life experience in heaven or hell. Although we should not seek supernatural experiences for the sake of seeking supernatural experiences, we should seek God and trust that He will give us what we need. There's nothing wrong with crying out to God to open your eyes when you sense that you aren't seeing what He really wants you to see.

In Elisha's day the king of Syria was warring against Israel. The prophet Elisha gave the Israelites a marked advantage—he was able to hear the words Syria's king spoke in his bedroom and relayed them to the king of Israel (2 Kings 6:12). The Syrian king wanted Elisha stopped and sent out horses and chariots and a great army to fetch him. When he saw the Syrian army that surrounded the city, Elisha's servant got scared:

> And his servant said to him, "Alas, my master! What will we do?" And he said, "Do not be afraid, for there are more with us than with them." Then Elisha prayed, "LORD, open his eyes and let him see." So the LORD opened the eyes of the young man, and he saw that the mountain was full of horses and chariots of fire surrounding Elisha.
>
> —2 KINGS 6:15–17

What confidence Elisha's servant must have gained—not just in that moment but also throughout his walk with the Lord. And that brings me to Paul's prayer for the church at Ephesus, which is something I would suggest praying over yourself daily. In this prayer Paul asks the Lord to open the believers' eyes for a specific purpose—a purpose that is sure to spark faith in soul and spirit:

> Therefore I also, after hearing of your faith in the Lord Jesus and your love toward all the saints, do not cease giving thanks for you, mentioning you in my prayers, so that the God of our Lord Jesus Christ, the Father of glory, may give you the Spirit of wisdom and revelation in the knowledge of Him, that the eyes of your understanding may be enlightened, that you may know what is the hope of His calling and what are the riches of the glory of His inheritance among the saints, and what is the surpassing greatness of His power toward us who believe, according to the working of His mighty power.
>
> —EPHESIANS 1:15–19

Powerful!

Again, although we should not seek supernatural experiences for the sake of seeking supernatural experiences—we should seek God, and He will give us what we need—there's nothing wrong with crying out to God to open your eyes when you sense that you aren't seeing what He really wants you to see. We all have blind spots, whether personal or with spiritual warfare. So cry out to God, ask Him to flood your heart with light—to open your eyes—and to show you what He wants you to see. Amen.

Rewards for Overcoming Jezebel

Bringing the balance discussion full circle, I do believe that Jezebel is one of the primary spirits coming against the church and operating in the world today. Just look around your city. How many tarot card readers, psychics, yoga shops, strip clubs, and smut stores do you see? Look at our nation, how many of our political and church leaders are falling into sexual immorality?

Jezebel's immoral, idolatrous influence surrounds us in the media as advertisers bombard us with sexually charged messages that try to convince us we can be thinner, smarter, or better looking, and get more of what we want from people because of it. Jezebel's puppets—Ahab, the false prophets, the eunuchs, and her spiritual children—are all around us to reinforce a false grace message that tolerates sin without repentance.

Jesus offers a clear reward to those who overcome Jezebel:

> Now to you I say, and to the rest in Thyatira, as many as do not have this doctrine, who have not known the depths of Satan, as they say, I will put on you no other burden. But hold fast what you have till I come. And he who overcomes, and keeps My works until the end, to him I will give power over the nations—"He shall rule them with a rod of iron; they shall be dashed to pieces like the potter's vessels"—as I also have received from My Father; and I will give him the morning star. He who has an ear, let him hear what the Spirit says to the churches.
>
> —Revelation 2:24–29, nkjv

Jesus is offering power over the nations and the morning star to the one who defeats the spirit of Jezebel. Power over the nations is fairly straightforward. You will have authority in this age and in the age to come. I can personally testify to the increase in spiritual authority and influence that the Lord offers in the wake of defeating Jezebel. Since my monumental battle with Jezebel that came to a victorious head in 2010, the Lord has given me a prophetic voice that has reached every nation of the earth.

But what is the "morning star"? I believe this is Christ Himself. Peter talks about the morning star, telling us that we have the prophetic word confirmed, "which you would do well to follow, as to a light that shines in a dark place, until the day dawns and the morning star arises in your hearts" (2 Pet. 1:19). Christ also refers to Himself with these words in the Book of Revelation: "I am the Root and the Offspring of David, the Bright and Morning Star" (Rev. 22:16).

In the days ahead I believe we're going to have to choose whom we will serve: Jezebel or Jesus. We will be rewarded according to our choice. If we side with Jezebel, we'll find judgment. If we side with Jesus, we'll receive authority and a revelation of His grace and glory. Let me leave you with the words of Joshua and a prayer:

> Now fear the LORD, and serve Him with sincerity and faithfulness. Put away the gods your fathers served beyond the River and in Egypt. Serve the LORD. If it is displeasing to you to serve the LORD, then choose today whom you will serve, if it should be the gods your fathers served beyond the River or the gods of the Amorites' land where you are now living. Yet as for me and my house, we will serve the LORD.
>
> —JOSHUA 24:14–15

Pray this with me:

Father, I come to you in the name of Jesus, and I ask you to give me discernment to recognize the spirits of Jezebel, Ahab, false prophets, eunuchs, and Jezebel's spiritual children influencing my life.

I repent, Lord, for aligning my heart with the spirit of this world that has distracted me from Your voice and Your love and allowed these spirits to work against Your purpose in my life. I break agreement with every spirit that is not of You, right now, in Your name. Please help me not to make snap judgments about spiritual warfare, but to discern the enemy's plot against me so that I can bind these assignments and walk free from the temptations Jezebel uses to capture my attention.

Give me a fresh revelation of my position and authority in Christ, His love for me, His spiritual armor, His blood, and His will. By Your grace, I commit to preserving my heart from the seducing, idolatrous, immoral agenda that Jezebel is forwarding in this age. Amen.

NOTES

Chapter 1
Satan's Fallen Angels

1. Biblestudytools.com, s.v. "*palé*," accessed August 25, 2015, http://www.biblestudytools.com/lexicons/greek/kjv/pale.html.

2. *Merriam-Webster's Collegiate Dictionary*, 11th edition (Springfield, MA: Merriam-Webster Inc., 2003), s. v. "stranglehold."

3. National Human Trafficking Resource Center, "National Human Trafficking Resource Center Annual Report," 2014, accessed August 26, 2015, http://www.traffickingresourcecenter.org/sites/default/files/2014%20NHTRC%20Annual%20Report_Final.pdf.

4. Human Rights Campaign, "2014 Municipal Equality Index Scorecard," accessed August 26, 2015, http://hrc-assets.s3-website-us-east-1.amazonaws.com//files/assets/resources/MEI-miamibeach-2014.pdf.

5. "America's Most Sinful Cities?", AlbertMohler.com, February 22, 2008, accessed August 26, 2015, http://www.albertmohler.com/2008/02/22/americas-most-sinful-cities/.

Chapter 2
Pulling the Mask Off Jezebel's Puppets

1. Encyclopedia Britannica, s.v. "Ahab," accessed July 24, 2015, http://www.britannica.com/biography/Ahab.

2. BibleHub.com, s.v. "Athaliah," accessed July 24, 2015, http://biblehub.com/topical/a/athaliah.htm.

3. BibleStudyTools.com, s.v. "Ahaziah," accessed July 24, 2015, http://www.biblestudytools.com/dictionary/ahaziah/.

4. BibleHub.com, s.v. "Jehoram," accessed July 24, 2015, http://biblehub.com/topical/j/jehoram.htm.

Chapter 3
Jezebel's Master Plot

1. Grace Unplugged, "About," accessed July 23, 2015, http://www.graceunplugged.com/about.
2. Peter Baker and John F. Harris, "Clinton Admits to Lewinsky Relationship, Challenges Starr to End Personal 'Prying,'" *Washington Post*, August 18, 1998, accessed July 24, 2015, http://www.washingtonpost.com/wp-srv/politics/special/clinton/stories/clinton081898.htm.

Chapter 4
Ahab the Empowerer

1. Biblestudytools.com, s.v. "beliyyaal," accessed September 1, 2015, http://www.biblestudytools.com/lexicons/hebrew/nas/beliyaal.html.
2. *Merriam-Webster's Collegiate Dictionary*, s.v. "codependency."
3. Mental Health America, "Passive-Aggressive Behavior," Orlando Health, accessed August 13, 2015, http://www.orlandohealth.com/conditions/passive-aggressive-behavior/.
4. Ibid.
5. Ibid.
6. Ibid.
7. Ibid.

Chapter 5
Unraveling Ahab's Alliances

1. Biblestudytools.com, s.v. "ethbaal," accessed September 1, 2015, http://www.biblestudytools.com/dictionary/ethbaal/.
2. Kent Worcester, *C. L. R. James: A Political Biography* (Albany, NY: State University Press of New York Press, 1996), 110.
3. Chris Woodward, "Barna: Many Pastors Wary of Raising 'Controversy,'" OneNewsNow, August 1, 2014, accessed October 29, 2015, http://onenewsnow.com/church/2014/08/01/barna-many-pastors-wary-of-raising-controversy.
4. Steve Sampson, *Discerning and Defeating the Ahab Spirit* (Grand Rapids, MI: Chosen, 2010), 16.

5. Mental Health America, "Co-Dependency," accessed July 23, 2015, http://www.mentalhealthamerica.net/co-dependency.

6. Jennifer LeClaire, "My Interview With Pastor Larry Huch on Breaking Generational Curses," Jennifer LeClaire Ministries, accessed July 24, 2015, http://www.jenniferleclaire.org/articles/my_interview_with_pastor_larry_huch_on_breaking_generational_curses.

Chapter 6
Jezebel's Yes-Men

1. *Merriam-Webster's Collegiate Dictionary*, s.v. "yes-man."

2. Joseph Benson, *Benson Commentary of the Old and New Testaments* (New York: T. Carlton & J. Porter, 1857); BibleHub.com, accessed July 23, 2015, http://biblehub.com/commentaries/1_kings/18-19.htm.

3. BibleHub.com, "Revelation 2:20," accessed July 23, 2015, http://biblehub.com/commentaries/jfb/revelation/2.htm.

4. BlueLetterBible.org, s.v. "*planaō*," accessed July 23, 2015, http://www.blueletterbible.org/lang/Lexicon/Lexicon.cfm?strongs=G4105&t=KJV.

5. BibleStudyTools.com, s.v. "*apoplanao*," accessed July 23, 2015, http://www.biblestudytools.com/lexicons/greek/nas/apoplanao.html; BibleStudyTools.com, s. v. "*apo*," accessed July 23, 2015, http://www.biblestudytools.com/lexicons/greek/nas/apo.html.

6. Alex Kocman, "Exclusive: Michael Brown Opens Up About His Upcoming Debate With Matthew Vines on 'Gay Christians,'" Charisma News, June 23, 2014, accessed July 23, 2015, http://www.charismanews.com/culture/44405-exclusive-michael-brown-opens-up-about-his-upcoming-debate-with-matthew-vines-about-gay-christians.

Chapter 8
The Royal Eunuchs

1. BibleTools.org, s.v. "*caryic*," accessed July 24, 2015, http://www.bibletools.org/index.cfm/fuseaction/Lexicon.show/ID/H5631/cariyc.htm.

2. Jennifer LeClaire, *Satan's Deadly Trio* (Grand Rapids, MI: Chosen Books, 2014).

3. Jennifer LeClaire, *The Heart of the Prophetic* (Hallandale, FL: Spirit of Life Publishing, 2007), 145.

Chapter 9
Escaping Spiritual Slavery

1. BibleStudyTools.com, s.v. "*baskaino*," accessed September 9, 2015, http://www.biblestudytools.com/lexicons/greek/nas/baskaino.html.

2. David Johnson and Jeff VanVonderen, *The Subtle Power of Spiritual Abuse* (Grand Rapids, MI: Bethany House, 2005); "Spiritual Abuse Recovery Resources," accessed August 13, 2015, http://www.spiritualabuse.com/.

3. Johnson and VanVonderen, *The Subtle Power of Spiritual Abuse*, 63.

4. Ibid., 67.

5. Ibid., 68.

Chapter 10
Recognizing Jezebel's Spiritual Children

1. BibleHub.com, s.v. "Athaliah," accessed July 24, 2015, http://biblehub.com/topical/a/athaliah.htm.

2. BibleHub.com, s.v. "2 Kings 11," accessed September 11, 2015, http://biblehub.com/commentaries/mhcw/2_kings/11.htm.

3. BibleStudyTools.com, "Ahaziah," accessed July 24, 2015, http://www.biblestudytools.com/dictionary/ahaziah/.

4. BibleHub.com, "Jehoram," accessed July 24, 2015, http://biblehub.com/topical/j/jehoram.htm.

Chapter 11
Giving Jezebel (and Her Children) Space to Repent

1. Blue Letter Bible, s.v. "*metanoeeō*," accessed September 11, 2015, http://www.blueletterbible.org/lang/Lexicon/Lexicon.cfm?strongs=G3340&t=KJV.

2. Charles G. Finney, *Lectures to Professing Christians* (New York: John S. Taylor, 1837), 119.

3. Ibid., 98.

4. Biblehub.com, s.v. "Revelation 2:22," accessed September 11, 2015, http://biblehub.com/nasb/revelation/2-22.htm.

5. Christian Classics Ethereal Library, s.v. "Revelation 2," accessed September 11, 2015, http://www.ccel.org/study/Revelation_2:26-27.

6. David Wilkerson, "The Doctrine of Jezebel!," January 18, 1988, World Challenge Pulpit Series, accessed July 23, 2015, http://www.tscpulpitseries.org/english/1980s/ts880118.html.

Chapter 13
Avoiding the Jehu Syndrome

1. Biblehub.com, s.v. "2 Kings 10:31," accessed September 11, 2015, http://biblehub.com/2_kings/10-31.htm.